RIBA Plan of Work 2013 Guide
Project Leadership

The RIBA Plan of Work 2013 Guides

Other titles in the series:

Design Management, by Dale Sinclair
Contract Administration, by Ian Davies
Town Planning, by Ruth Reed

Coming in 2015:

Information Exchanges
Sustainability
Conservation
Health and Safety
Handover Strategy

The RIBA Plan of Work 2013 is endorsed by the following organisations:

Royal Incorporation of Architects in Scotland	Chartered Institute of Architectural Technologists	Royal Society of Architects in Wales	Construction Industry Council	Royal Society of Ulster Architects

RIBA Plan of Work 2013 Guide

Project Leadership

Nick Willars

RIBA ☷ **Publishing**

© RIBA Enterprises Ltd, 2014
Published by RIBA Publishing, The Old Post Office, St Nicholas Street,
Newcastle upon Tyne NE1 1RH

ISBN 978 1 85946 51 6
Stock code 82651

The right of Nick Willars to be identified as the Author of this Work has
been asserted in accordance with the Copyright, Designs and Patents
Act 1988 sections 77 and 78.

British Library Cataloguing in Publication Data
A catalogue record for this book is available from the British Library.

Commissioning Editor: Sarah Busby
Series Editor: Dale Sinclair
Project Manager: Alasdair Deas
Design: Kneath Associates
Typesetting: Academic+Technical, Bristol, UK
Printed and bound by CPI Group (UK) Ltd
Cover image: © Michèle Woodger

Picture credits
The following figures are reproduced with permission: 0.2: Hatfield
Consultants (hatfieldgroup.com); 1.6, 1.7, 2.1, 2.4, 2.5, 2.6, 3.2, 3.3, 3.5,
4.3: Buro Four; 2.2: Eva Jiricna Architects; 2.3: Adjaye Associates;
3.1: Mark Bew and Mervyn Richards; 4.1: X6 (Beijing) Architecture and
Engineering Consulting Co Ltd; 7.1: Swanke Hayden Connell Architects

While every effort has been made to check the accuracy and quality
of the information given in this publication, neither the Author nor the
Publisher accept any responsibility for the subsequent use of this
information, for any errors or omissions that it may contain, or for any
misunderstandings arising from it.

RIBA Publishing is part of RIBA Enterprises Ltd
www.ribaenterprises.com

Contents

Foreword

Having had many discussions on the subject of managing the design process with Nick Willars during our years working together at Buro Four, I was delighted when he rang me to tell me that he was writing a publication entitled *Project Leadership*. My reasons were twofold: first, Nick is probably one of the best, if not the best, people qualified to tackle such a task and, second, such a reference document for the property and construction industry is at least a couple of decades overdue. My own experience of working closely for and with design teams is testament to this lack of sound guidance and, having read the first proof, I view this work as an essential reference document for any professional already in the project lead role, as well as for any aspiring project lead. The publication should also be on the library shelf of every design and construction organisation which considers itself capable of undertaking sizable and complex projects or programmes of work.

As I read the guide I noted my comments and the key aspects I thought to be of greatest value to users. On reviewing my notes I realised that simply summarising my comments was probably the most appropriate way to explain my enthusiasm for the completed work and its value to any potential reader. So, in no particular order of priority:

I It is a complete guide for any professional who is charged with being the project lead at any or all stages of a project.
I It sets out to identify and define each stage of a project and describes the skills required to successfully navigate each aspect of every stage.
I The first stage starts by describing how to ensure that the client's Business Case is solidly built into the foundations of the project. One can see that it may take a day, a week, a month or even a year to complete this stage before the next stage can be contemplated, let alone Concept Design. This is an area that is too often signed off or presented without having been fully considered or interrogated.
I The 'in-text features' (examples; tools and templates; signposts; hints and tips) give dozens of great pointers and reminders to the issues that will need to be fully considered and resolved.

I The guidance is not prescriptive – it allows the project lead to design a plan that reflects the client's individual stage and project objectives, as well as the nature and complexity of the project.

I Reading the introduction to each section (or stage) just before the start of a stage serves as a great reminder of 'what's coming up', whether you are taking on or taking over the project leadership.

I Reading each section will help the reader to assess whether they have both the technical skills and the leadership qualities needed and, indeed, where support may be required.

I It contains an in-text feature that highlights variations in approach for smaller projects.

During my career I have informally mentored a number of architects on the subject of managing (or leading) the design. They will have heard me say 'just put down your pencil, we're not ready to start the design yet'. This is more elegantly put by Nick Willars as 'understand the question before you start to answer it'. Taking on board the wisdom, experience and guidance contained in this guide will save a lot of time and effort in successfully delivering projects.

Eva Jiricna's creativity process, shown in figure 2.2 (or what, more often than not, generally occurs during RIBA Stages 0, 1 and 2), will, I believe, be straightened by some measure as a direct result of project leads making use of this guide.

Clive Birch Hon. FRIBA, Oct. 2014
Co-founder of Buro Four
External examiner, University College London

Series editor's foreword

The RIBA Plan of Work 2013 was developed in response to the needs of an industry adjusting to emerging digital design processes, disruptive technologies and new procurement models, as well as other drivers. A core challenge is to communicate the thinking behind the new RIBA Plan in greater detail. This process is made more complex because the RIBA Plan of Work has existed for 50 years and is embodied within the psyche and working practices of everyone involved in the built environment sector. Its simplicity has allowed it to be interpreted and used in many ways, underpinning the need to explain the content of the Plan's first significant edit. By relating the Plan to a number of commonly encountered topics, the *RIBA Plan of Work 2013 Guides* series forms a core element of the communication strategy and I am delighted to be acting as the series editor.

The first strategic shift in the RIBA Plan of Work 2013 was to acknowledge a change from the tasks of the design team to those of the project team: the client, design team and contractor. Stages 0 and 7 are part of this shift, acknowledging that buildings are used by clients, or their clients, and, more importantly, recognising the paradigm shift from designing for construction towards the use of high-quality design information to help facilitate better whole-life outcomes.

New procurement strategies focused around assembling the right project team are the beginnings of significant adjustments in the way that buildings will be briefed, designed, constructed, operated and used. Design teams are harnessing new digital design technologies (commonly bundled under the BIM wrapper), linking geometric information to new engineering analysis software to create a generation of buildings that would not previously have been possible. At the same time, coordination processes and environmental credentials are being improved. A core focus is the progressive fixity of high-quality information – for the first time, the right information at the right time, clearly defining who does what, when.

The RIBA Plan of Work 2013 aims to raise the knowledge bar on many subjects, including sustainability, Information Exchanges and health and safety. The *RIBA Plan of Work 2013 Guides* are crucial tools in disseminating and explaining how these themes are fully addressed and how the new Plan can be harnessed to achieve the new goals and objectives of our clients.

Dale Sinclair
November 2014

Acknowledgements and dedication

I would like to thank Georgina Stobart and Katriona Greenhorn, both members of the AECOM design management team, who made invaluable contributions to the first and last chapters of this book respectively. Thanks also go to Sahar Saad, also from AECOM, who helped me with some essential administrative tasks.

I would also like to thank the directors of Buro Four for supporting me through the early stages of the book and providing me with the opportunities to experience much of the subject matter at first hand during my time leading the Buro Four Design Management group.

I'd like to thank Heather, Carla and Robyn for putting up with countless weekends with me sitting at the computer instead of DIY, housework, shopping or gardening.

Finally, I'd like to thank Sarah Busby and Dale Sinclair for their constant encouragement in maintaining the momentum towards looming deadlines and for their valuable input into the publication.

About the author

Nick Willars is a qualified architect, project manager and design manager. He is currently Director of Design Management at AECOM, looking after their multidisciplinary design management service. He has over 20 years' experience as an architect in the private sector encompassing design, client liaison, resourcing, programming and strategy delivery in a diverse range of sectors. Previously he has been involved in the successful delivery of several high profile and award winning projects in both the UK and the Far East for Terry Farrell & Partners. He led the education sector for Swanke Hayden Connell Architects before joining Buro Four in 2007 to lead the design management team. He has substantial technical knowledge of the processes involved in design management and the coordination of large consultant teams and has extensive experience of collaborative working with high profile clients and major contractors on complex projects both at home and overseas. Nick is also a member of the RIBA's Construction Leadership Group.

About the series editor

Dale Sinclair is Director of Technical Practice for AECOM's architecture team in EMEA. He is an architect and was previously a director at Dyer and an associate director at BDP. He has taught at Aberdeen University and the Mackintosh School of Architecture and regularly lectures on BIM, design management and the RIBA Plan of Work 2013. He is passionate about developing new design processes that can harness digital technologies, manage the iterative design process and improve design outcomes.

He is currently the RIBA Vice President, Practice and Profession, a trustee of the RIBA Board, a UK board member of BuildingSMART and a member of various CIC working groups. He was the editor of the *BIM Overlay to the Outline Plan of Work 2007*, edited the RIBA Plan of Work 2013 and was author of its supporting tools and guidance publications: *Guide to Using the RIBA Plan of Work 2013* and *Assembling the Collaborative Project Team*.

Introduction

Overview

This book is intended to provide guidance to the potential project lead and describes the objectives and activities required to help the design team navigate through the process outlined in the RIBA Plan of Work 2013 from Stage 0 (Strategic Definition) to Stage 7 (In Use).

The project lead role is not specific to any particular discipline within the design team and could be the project manager or the lead designer. The lead designer could be the architect or, in certain circumstances, on infrastructure projects the role could be assumed by the structural or services engineer. The project lead is therefore not specified in the text but it must be understood that the role at every stage should be undertaken by the most appropriate individual with the right personality, experience and leadership skills to gain the respect and trust of both the client and the design team.

This introduction expands on some of the generic qualities expected of the project lead, how to adopt a leadership approach rather than just a management role and some of the key issues that will contribute to the success of a project across all stages.

Context

The most important aspect of project leadership is the adoption of a 'one team, one goal' approach. Collaboration is the key to progress and the adoption of collective responsibility in the delivery of project within a 'no blame' culture will promote success. Encouraging client participation and engagement will help the design team to head in the right direction and, by instigating progressive approvals at appropriate milestones, the project lead will help to minimise wasted time and resources.

The project lead should ensure that a clear and coordinated set of professional services agreements are prepared at the outset to engender a mutual understanding of each other's roles and responsibilities, which will help to minimise conflict and disruption. However, while the principle of 'everyone doing their job' can be successful, it rarely results in the true added value that the collaborative approach can deliver. In adverse situations, individuals within the client's team can sometimes resort to practising the opposite approach of 'divide and rule'. This approach may be in line with the ethos of certain organisations and cultures but will rarely result in the development of a long-term or repeated relationship based on trust and respect. Ultimately, selecting the right personnel, who are willing to embrace the above culture, will be a significant contributing factor to the success of the project.

The project lead will also be instrumental in clearly communicating not only the 'what' and the 'when' but also the 'how': this ensures that all contributors, including the client, understand the commitment required to contribute to the process and are therefore able to buy in to the content, programme and methodology for the delivery of the design.

A comprehensive Initial Project Brief that provides a clear set of client requirements will help the design team to focus on the design response with minimal misinterpretation and iterations. Inclusive project planning, identifying the rationale behind the interim milestones and clarifying the objectives will help the design team to understand the difference between design development and variations, whether instigated by the client or the design team members themselves.

The project lead must get to know the client organisation and really understand its personality, approach, priorities and culture of work. Combining this with a thorough appreciation of a project's unique requirements is essential to enable the design team to deliver not only the best value on a given project, but also the optimum service for the client.

How to use this book

The chapter headings follow the sequence of the RIBA Plan of Work 2013, with each chapter expanding on the responsibilities and activities expected of the project lead at that particular stage of the project. However, the plan is not prescriptive and, dependent on the scale, location and complexity of a given project together with the procurement strategy, some of the activities and objectives will overlap stages. Early involvement of the contractor will also add another dimension to the project team and the project lead will have to ensure that the approach adopted by the design team is also adopted by the contractor; this will help to avoid a divergence of the project culture and potential conflict in ideology.

It will be necessary for the project lead to communicate the strategies and management methodologies through the introduction of a variety of project tools and systems. Some of those are described in the following chapters. However, the systems and processes put in place by the project lead will only be effective if the project lead adopts a consistent approach with both the client and the design team, demonstrating total and clear commitment. By listening, including others and offering support where required, the project lead will inspire a strong team ethos, a high level of commitment and a 'can-do' mentality from all members of the project team.

Nick Willars
November 2014

Using this series

For ease of reference each book in this series is broken down into chapters that map on to the stages of the Plan of Work. So, for instance, the first chapter covers the tasks and considerations around project leadership at Stage 0.

We have also included several in-text features to enhance your understanding of the topic. The following key will explain what each icon means and why each feature is useful to you:

 The 'Example' feature explores an example from practice, either real or theoretical

 The 'Tools and Templates' feature outlines standard tools, letters and forms and how to use them in practice

 The 'Signpost' feature introduces you to further sources of trusted information from books, websites and regulations

 The 'Definition' feature explains key terms in this topic area in more detail

 The 'Hints and Tips' feature dispenses pragmatic advice and highlights common problems and solutions

 The 'Small Project Observation' feature highlights useful variations in approach and outcome for smaller projects

RIBA ⚜

The **RIBA Plan of Work 2013** organises the process of briefing, designing, constructing, maintaining, operating and using building projects into a number of key stages. The content of stages may vary or overlap to suit specific project requirements.

RIBA Plan of Work 2013

Tasks ▼	**0** Strategic Definition	**1** Preparation and Brief	**2** Concept Design	**3** Developed Design
Core Objectives	Identify client's **Business Case** and **Strategic Brief** and other core project requirements.	Develop **Project Objectives**, including **Quality Objectives** and **Project Outcomes**, **Sustainability Aspirations**, **Project Budget**, other parameters or constraints and develop **Initial Project Brief**. Undertake **Feasibility Studies** and review of **Site Information**.	Prepare **Concept Design**, including outline proposals for structural design, building services systems, outline specifications and preliminary **Cost Information** along with relevant **Project Strategies** in accordance with **Design Programme**. Agree alterations to brief and issue **Final Project Brief**.	Prepare **Developed Design**, including coordinated and updated proposals for structural design, building services systems, outline specifications, **Cost Information** and **Project Strategies** in accordance with **Design Programme**.
Procurement *Variable task bar	Initial considerations for assembling the project team.	Prepare **Project Roles Table** and **Contractual Tree** and continue assembling the project team.	← The procurement strategy does not fundamentally alter the progression of the design or the level of detail prepared at	a given stage. However, **Information Exchanges** will vary depending on the selected procurement route and **Building Contract**. A bespoke **RIBA Plan of Work**
Programme *Variable task bar	Establish **Project Programme**.	Review **Project Programme**.	Review **Project Programme**.	← The procurement route may dictate the **Project Programme** and result in certain stages overlapping
(Town) Planning *Variable task bar	Pre-application discussions.	Pre-application discussions.	← Planning applications are typically made using the Stage 3 output.	A bespoke **RIBA Plan of Work 2013** will identify when the
Suggested Key Support Tasks	Review **Feedback** from previous projects.	Prepare **Handover Strategy** and **Risk Assessments**. Agree **Schedule of Services**, **Design Responsibility Matrix** and **Information Exchanges** and prepare **Project Execution Plan** including **Technology** and **Communication Strategies** and consideration of **Common Standards** to be used.	Prepare **Sustainability Strategy, Maintenance and Operational Strategy** and review **Handover Strategy** and **Risk Assessments**. Undertake third party consultations as required and any **Research and Development** aspects. Review and update **Project Execution Plan**. Consider **Construction Strategy**, including offsite fabrication, and develop **Health and Safety Strategy**.	Review and update **Sustainability, Maintenance and Operational** and **Handover Strategies** and **Risk Assessments**. Undertake third party consultations as required and conclude **Research and Development** aspects. Review and update **Project Execution Plan**, including **Change Control Procedures**. Review and update **Construction** and **Health and Safety Strategies**.
Sustainability Checkpoints	**Sustainability Checkpoint — 0**	**Sustainability Checkpoint — 1**	**Sustainability Checkpoint — 2**	**Sustainability Checkpoint — 3**
Information Exchanges (at stage completion)	**Strategic Brief.**	**Initial Project Brief.**	**Concept Design** including outline structural and building services design, associated **Project Strategies**, preliminary **Cost Information** and **Final Project Brief**.	**Developed Design**, including the coordinated architectural, structural and building services design and updated **Cost Information**.
UK Government Information Exchanges	Not required.	Required.	Required.	Required.

*Variable task bar – in creating a bespoke project or practice specific RIBA Plan of Work 2013 via www.ribaplanofwork.com a specific bar is selected from a number of options.

The **RIBA Plan of Work 2013** should be used solely as guidance for the preparation of detailed professional services contracts and building contracts.

www.ribaplanofwork.com

4 Technical Design	**5** Construction	**6** Handover and Close Out	**7** In Use
Prepare **Technical Design** in accordance with **Design Responsibility Matrix** and **Project Strategies** to include all architectural, structural and building services information, specialist subcontractor design and specifications, in accordance with **Design Programme**.	Offsite manufacturing and onsite **Construction** in accordance with **Construction Programme** and resolution of **Design Queries** from site as they arise.	Handover of building and conclusion of **Building Contract**.	Undertake **In Use** services in accordance with **Schedule of Services**.
2013 will set out the specific tendering and procurement activities that will occur at each stage in relation to the chosen procurement route.	Administration of **Building Contract**, including regular site inspections and review of progress.	Conclude administration of **Building Contract**.	
or being undertaken concurrently. A bespoke **RIBA Plan of Work 2013** will clarify the stage overlaps.	The **Project Programme** will set out the specific stage dates and detailed programme durations.		
planning application is to be made.			
Review and update **Sustainability, Maintenance and Operational** and **Handover Strategies** and **Risk Assessments**. Prepare and submit Building Regulations submission and any other third party submissions requiring consent. Review and update **Project Execution Plan**. Review **Construction Strategy**, including sequencing, and update **Health and Safety Strategy**.	Review and update **Sustainability Strategy** and implement **Handover Strategy**, including agreement of information required for commissioning, training, handover, asset management, future monitoring and maintenance and ongoing compilation of **'As-constructed' Information**. Update **Construction** and **Health and Safety Strategies**.	Carry out activities listed in **Handover Strategy** including **Feedback** for use during the future life of the building or on future projects. Updating of **Project Information** as required.	Conclude activities listed in **Handover Strategy** including **Post-occupancy Evaluation**, review of **Project Performance, Project Outcomes** and **Research and Development** aspects. Updating of **Project Information**, as required, in response to ongoing client **Feedback** until the end of the building's life.
Sustainability Checkpoint — 4	**Sustainability Checkpoint — 5**	**Sustainability Checkpoint — 6**	**Sustainability Checkpoint — 7**
Completed **Technical Design** of the project.	**'As-constructed' Information**.	Updated **'As-constructed' Information**.	**'As-constructed' Information** updated in response to ongoing client **Feedback** and maintenance or operational developments.
Not required.	Not required.	Required.	As required.

© RIBA

Stage 0

Strategic Definition

Chapter overview

Stage 0 (Strategic Definition) is a key stage as it identifies the business justification for a building project and who needs to be involved. This chapter will detail the parallel activities for the project lead to consider, ensuring that the best use of time is made during this vital part of the pre-design stage. It will also examine the responsibilities that the project lead should take on at this stage and common mistakes to try to avoid.

The key coverage in this chapter is as follows:

Core Objectives

Project lead attributes

Developing the Business Case

Articulating the Strategic Brief

Vision statement

Stakeholder identification

Initial appointments

Client-appointed advisers

Sustainability Aspirations

Project Programme

Detailed Plan of Work for next stage

Introduction

Stage 0 represents the beginning of the project and the need for the client to understand and justify the Business Case. There are countless requirements that can influence a client's decision to undertake a project and it is the project lead's responsibility to ensure that these have been properly considered and that the most appropriate path is followed to satisfy these requirements and generate the Strategic Brief.

What are the Core Objectives of this stage?

The Core Objectives of the RIBA Plan of Work 2013 at Stage 0 are:

The Core Objective of this stage is to realise and articulate the client's Business Case, the Strategic Brief and to identify other relevant core project requirements. This process should clarify the overall aspirations and expectations for the project.

Project lead attributes

It is worth considering at the outset the role and responsibilities of the project lead. During the Strategic Definition stage of a project the client may not have appointed any members of the design team as they may have the resources in-house to provide the necessary expertise to commence the process of defining the project need. Whether or not this is the case, it will be necessary for the client to select, either internally or from an external consultancy, an individual with the appropriate attributes to lead the process and organise the required participants in a structured manner, providing a clear understanding of the objectives and activities in order to set the scene for the lengthy and complex process that will follow.

The project lead must:

I have a demonstrable understanding of how to identify, programme and allocate the key activities
I be able to organise the participation and encourage the commitment of appropriate contributors to steer these activities towards the pre-agreed objectives of each stage
I be able to map out a relevant and efficient process for the design team to follow
I be collaborative in their approach to decision making
I have excellent communication skills
I have a first hand understanding of the design process
I have sufficient experience to understand the implications of each decision as it is made.

There are no set rules dictating which discipline the individual who will adopt the project lead role will come from and it will vary from project to project depending on size, complexity and the discipline most suited to the nature of the project. The likely candidates, however, are:

I the lead designer (could be the architect or engineer)
I the project manager
I the client representative
I the contractor (especially in public–private partnership projects).

Lead designer

On most building projects, the lead designer is usually the architect, unless the project is infrastructure or highly serviced. The role is predominantly about defining the design process from inception to completion and, where there is no design manager, communicating and managing that process. As the name suggests, the lead designer is also the party responsible for developing the design and coordinating the inputs of all members of the design team and for liaising with the client on issues relating to design.

Although the project lead will have to make key decisions at all stages of the process, they will not be acting alone and must use the experience of both the client and the appointed participants to create an environment that avoids unilateral direction and encourages more collaborative working from the assembled expert project team.

It is the job of the project lead to give clear and timely structured guidance and mentoring to the client to ensure that they are able to function and participate in a way that contributes to the design process and ultimately the success of the project.

Developing the Business Case

For projects of any scale, the development of a Business Case is essential to ensure that a project obtains the initial high-level approval to commence. Whether the client is reporting to a board, to shareholders or even if they themselves are the main decision maker in the company, the project lead's role is to help the client provide a clear justification of the value that the project will bring. This value is most often linked to direct financial returns but can also be linked to sustainability, societal or branding benefits, which can be more difficult to directly quantify. Either way, the Business Case must consider all of these elements as well as the opportunities and risks that present themselves and link them to the overall requirement for the client's operations.

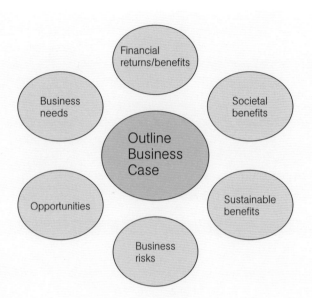

Figure 0.1   Business Case considerations

Small project at Stage 0

The Business Case is therefore also crucial on a small project, as it not only establishes the methods by which the project will be funded but also provides a clear justification for the project and the criteria by which its success can be measured. It outlines the business need – the operational aspirations of the project from which the design team will be able to establish the accommodation and relationships necessary to ensure that the building functions as required.

Capital expenditure vs operating costs

A key part of any Business Case is in the consideration of the balance between capital expenditure (CapEx) and operating costs/expenditure (OpEx). Most companies/clients will be familiar with this particular challenge and the decisions regarding funding can be influenced by a number of factors, not least initial accessibility of capital and funding mechanisms or whether the project is to be occupied by the developer or client and also the anticipated design life of the building. To assess the last issue, a project lead will often ensure that a life cycle cost assessment (LCCA) is prepared to calculate the overall cost of ownership of the building or development based on various business options presented.

Life cycle assessment

A technique that asses the total life cycle costs and maintenance requirements of a project from inception to eventual demolition.

Existing workplace

It is not surprising that a client will often initiate a project with the preconceived idea that they require a new building to satisfy their expanding needs and fail to properly consider the adaptability potential of their existing space.

Is a new building necessary?

A client may think that in order to accommodate their growing business they have to build a new office. However, following assessment of the existing space they may decide to spend capital on a more efficient space planning approach or alternative operational strategies to satisfy the perceived need for extra space.

This can be a far more efficient and financially beneficial approach, which is often overlooked when considering the options available within the Business Case. This approach will also result in a more sustainable future if considered at the outset of all projects.

This is a key consideration of the project justification at the outset as later challenges to the client's requirements will inevitably prove extremely disruptive and costly, both commercially and in terms of wasted resources and effort.

Physical vs operational

Another alternative approach is for the client to assess during the Strategic Definition stage whether there are opportunities to enhance operational capabilities by increasing the number of employees or upgrading existing equipment rather than committing to the expansion of accommodation by initiating a new project.

Alternatives to expansion?

A factory owner may consider investing capital in expanding their premises to accommodate additional machinery that will increase their output levels but may find that it is more cost effective to increase the number of workers, who may be able to provide the same level of output. This is particularly applicable in regions where the cost of increasing the number of personnel is lower than that of purchasing technology.

Again, the project lead must exhaust all possibilities that could later undermine the justification for a new project.

Articulating the Strategic Brief

The Strategic Brief represents the first interpretation of the Business Case to begin to define the client's requirements in respect of project objectives and space needs. At this point, the Business Case has identified the business requirements and desired value which the client wants to achieve but the development of the Strategic Brief involves developing these requirements to a level of detail that will allow for the preparation of the Initial Project Brief. This is described in more detail in the next chapter.

Project Objectives

The Project Objectives are established in collaboration with the client at the outset of a project to identify the essential driving forces behind the aesthetic, functional and operational aspects of the project.

It is at this stage that the project lead should consider looking beyond the immediate client and begin to engage with relevant stakeholders and specialist consultants. Although it is vital that this exercise remains client-led and driven, engaging these groups at this early stage offers the dual benefit of sourcing valuable input into the detail of the brief, thanks to their day-to-day understanding of the operational business needs, and encouraging collective ownership of the content of the Strategic Brief.

A common mistake for the project lead to avoid is the temptation to plunge into detailed solutions to the requirements identified in the Business Case rather than refining these requirements to a greater level of detail to form a baseline summary of the needs as part of the Project Brief. This process is discussed in more detail in the next chapter.

Vision statement

The development of a vision or 'mission' statement is an effective way to communicate the core themes or goals of a project to the wider team. A vision statement can vary in the degree of specific detail and the project lead should determine what is most appropriate for the type of project being undertaken.

Vision statement

For the 2012 London Olympic and Paralympic Games the overall vision was to 'inspire a generation'. Due to the scale of this event, this could be interpreted as inspiring a generation athletically, architecturally or personally but the core purpose was defined in such a way that all these elements were reflected across all aspects of the Games.

However, not many projects will find such a broad-ranging approach sufficient to communicate the vision and therefore more specific values may need to be embedded in the mission statement. Refining a vision statement to suit an individual project also gives the project lead the opportunity to link relevant metrics and methods of measuring achievement of these values in later stages, as shown in the example below.

Vision statement: '*Maximise the **use of capital** and **innovation** to create a **productive** and **healthy working environment** with **low long-term operating costs** and **strong environmentally sustainable performance**.*'

Table 0.1   *Methods of measuring achievement*

CRITERIA	CONCEPT	METRIC	MEASUREMENT
Use of capital	Value	Cost of achieving all other objectives	Empirical: build/OpEx cost per m^2
Innovation	Process efficiency and technical efficiency	Performance against budget cost, building performance and schedule targets	Against reference projects
Productive	Building efficiency	Space use per head Space quality and efficiency	Work outputs, employee feedback
Healthy	Air and environmental quality for occupants	Indoor air quality	Employee health and wellbeing surveys, number of sick days
Low operating costs	Investment	OpEx costs	Assessment of operational costs against set benchmarks
Environmentally sustainable performance	Best practice in sustainable building design	Achievement of BREAAM credits	Achievement of desired BREAAM rating score

Vision for a small project

Small projects will generally also have a vision, which will act as an overarching guide to the design team in periodically testing the response to check that the vision is intact. This could be as simple as the client's desire 'to live a clutter-free existence' or stating 'natural light is everything to me' – neither are specific but both are measurable as the design unfolds.

Stakeholder identification

During Stage 0, the project lead should attempt to identify all relevant stakeholders on the project. Although it is often difficult to foresee the various stakeholders at this early stage, this aspect needs to be considered with the client representative from the outset so that the team can develop a plan to ensure appropriate interaction with these people/groups throughout the different stages.

Initially, it is probably best to cast a wide net when considering who the stakeholders on a project might be and it is usually helpful to consider the following questions:

I Who has influence (eg ability to provide regulatory approvals, funding, etc.)?
I What physical interfaces (utilities, transport etc.) are there with the project?
I Who will be using or operating the space?
I Who might have a strong interest in the project?
I Who will be affected (directly/indirectly) by the project?

It is advisable to speak to those who have worked on similar projects or in the same geographical area in the past for input and consider any approvals or permits the project may require. Once a list is developed and if the project scale warrants it, the project lead should classify these various stakeholders into one of the four categories shown in figure 0.2.

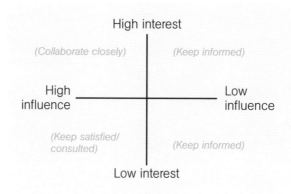

Figure 0.2   Stakeholder categorisation

Stakeholders with opinions but no authority

It is important that the project lead understands the level of authority of every stakeholder and that their interface with the wider team is properly managed and controlled. For example, it can be problematic when an end user of the space makes requests for improvements or developments to the project brief directly to the design team without considering the commercial and contractual implications that these demands may present. Therefore, there will be a need to designate an individual within the organisation to act as a point of contact for stakeholders and ensure that any feedback or requests are formalised so there is no confusion over what constitutes a formal instruction and what items fall under a given stakeholder's 'wish list'.

By categorising these stakeholders, an approach for managing these groups/people can be developed to ensure that the team is engaging with the appropriate people who have the appropriate level of authority at the right stage of the project.

Initial appointments

As mentioned earlier in the chapter, the Strategic Definition of a project may not involve a great number of external project team members, as the client may have appropriate expertise in-house to meet the objectives of this stage. However, the client should understand that the decisions they take during this stage will require a degree of expertise in project delivery to avoid time-consuming and costly challenges and revalidation by a complete design team later in the process. The project lead (whether internal or external) will appreciate this from the outset and should advise the client of gaps in expert advice that could affect the definition of the project and ultimately affect the briefing and design process.

So, it is clear that someone must lead this initial process for the client, and recognise and identify the expertise required to properly justify and define the project. This could be the project manager or the lead designer depending on the scale, complexity and typology of the project. Smaller projects will be lead by the lead designer or architect as they have all the necessary skills to perform the role. Larger projects are onerous in terms of their technical challenges, complex management procedures and high level of multidisciplinary coordination required and could warrant the involvement of an expert project manager to facilitate and navigate the process in order to allow the lead designer or architect to concentrate on content and design. Major infrastructure projects, for example, may be best lead by a civil engineer.

Client-appointed advisers

There will often be a need for the client to appoint various advisers who will be required to identify the project need during Stage 0. The type of adviser will be largely dependent on the type of project and the degree of internal resources to which the client has access. However, these advisers will often provide input in terms of legal issues, insurance, public relations and branding. It is the responsibility of the project lead to identify how these advisers, and the advice they provide, are integrated into the project process.

Sustainability Aspirations

In recent times, it has become commonplace to see a strong emphasis placed on environmental sustainability in design and construction projects. However, there is a broad spectrum in terms of identifying just how influential these Sustainability Aspirations should be and the project lead must assess how well they gel with the main goals of the project and the degree to which the client will compromise issues, such as capital outlay, in achieving these aspirations.

A range of sustainability rating systems is available throughout the world, each with different methods of assessing a project's performance. The most commonly used design and assessment method in the UK is BREEAM, whereas the LEED certification programme is most prominent in the US, along with several other rating tools that are widely recognised in other countries.

As far as possible, the high-level aspiration for sustainability should be established early in the process and be included in the Strategic Brief for further development within the emerging Initial Project Brief.

Site selection

An example where early consideration of sustainability targeting is important relates to the selection of the site and its existing ecological value. If the site for a project is not yet confirmed, it is worth factoring in the potential to achieve credits during site selection in the decision-making process.

Site selection is one example where credits can be achieved with minimal effort by assessing the required credits at the outset of the project and making timely decisions to optimise the ability to score highly.

For further reading on design and assessment methods for sustainable buildings visit the BREEAM website at www.breeam.org/

Project Programme

At Stage 0 of a project, the project lead should develop a very high-level Project Programme to communicate the expected timeframe for the main stages of the project. Usually this can be simplified into the following three elements:

1. Design
2. Procurement
3. Construction.

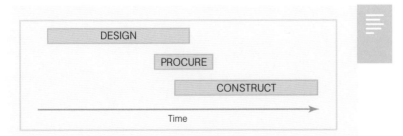

Figure 0.3   High-level outline Project Programme

This can be shown on a basic Gantt chart diagram, which sets the overall time period for the project to be developed with additional detailed activities added during the later stages. The Project Programme is discussed in more detail during the following chapters.

Detailed Plan of Work for next stage

The final requirement for a project lead at the end of Stage 0 is to select the right project team for Stage 1 and ensure that the objectives and activities of this stage are properly defined. Therefore, it is useful to set out a list of objectives, which filter down into defined deliverables to be achieved in the following stage to ensure that a clear shift in focus is defined for the transition between stages.

Chapter summary 0

This first stage in the RIBA Plan of Work 2013 needs careful consideration by all those involved to ensure that the Business Case and Strategic Brief are developed through careful exploration of the overall needs of the client. A clear understanding of the drivers and justification of the project must be considered from the outset to ensure that these aspirations are successfully communicated to the design team, allowing it to focus its efforts on a pre-agreed set of requirements.

To do this, the client's Project Objectives must be clearly captured, justified and communicated to all those who need to be involved, whether client-appointed advisers, client stakeholders or third party interests. An appropriately experienced project lead must be identified and, if necessary, brought in to facilitate this process in order to ensure that the scene is set correctly at the outset to avoid unnecessary disruption later in the design process

Preparation and Brief

Chapter overview

Stage 1 Preparation and Brief is possibly the most commonly misinterpreted stage for designers. This chapter aims to set out the key activities and responsibilities for the project lead in support of the Core Objectives of the stage.

The key coverage in this chapter is as follows:

Core Objectives

Design strategy

The project team

The Initial Project Brief

Project Budget

Project Programme

Procurement

Common building contracts

Project Execution Plan

Site Information

Feasibility Studies

Risk Assessments

Introduction

Stage 1 essentially provides the opportunity to make sure the client has considered the optimum balance of content/quality/cost/time for the project. The client must incorporate this information into an Initial Project Brief and test those assumptions to prove that, at a strategic level, the Initial Project Brief can be delivered. Therefore, this stage is about identifying the need, defining the parameters that support the client's Business Case and ostensibly asking the 'question' to which the design team can formulate a response in the following stages.

The temptation to start sketching design solutions at this stage is overwhelming for many designers and the project lead's role in establishing the overarching objectives of this stage at the outset will be critical to the efficiency and proper sequencing of the activities required during the following stages. Design should be limited to validating the Project Brief, which may take the form of statements, schedules or sketches. However, the sketching at this stage should only be in the form of Feasibility Studies to prove that the brief is deliverable. These could involve testing whether the site is of sufficient size to take a building of the requisite area without exceeding height constraints; this stage is not about how the building will look other than as massing or stacking diagrams.

What are the Core Objectives of this stage?

The Core Objectives of the RIBA Plan of Work 2013 at Stage 1 are:

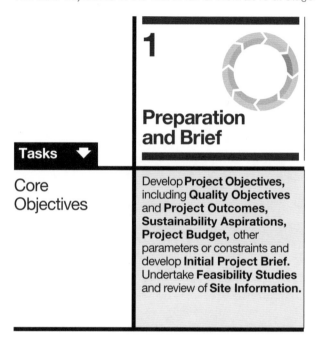

The Core Objective of this stage is to make sure that, in collaboration with the client, the design team has a clear understanding of the client's objectives, starting with a vision that aligns with the client's Business Case as discussed in the previous chapter. Having established this, the goal is to produce an Initial Project Brief that has been properly tested through Feasibility Studies which properly demonstrate the viability of the Initial Project Brief. This means that, before entering Stage 2 Concept Design, the design team knows that at a strategic level both they and the client have a clear understanding of what is being asked for and therefore what they are responding to but, more importantly, that there are likely to be one or more viable design solutions that meet the client's requirements within the constraints established in the Initial Project Brief.

Design strategy

The design strategy describes the method by which the design information will be executed and therefore could potentially affect the programme, the design responsibilities and the roles of members of the design team and also the quality of the contract information.

The direction of the design strategy will vary depending on the size and complexity of a project. On larger, more complex projects the project lead will have to consider, as a minimum, whether the conceptual designer is best placed to execute the detailed design or whether specialist executive designers should be appointed to take the responsibility. In most projects, the default strategy will be to retain the original Concept Design team until completion of the contract information but, even in this case, there will be areas of the design where the risk associated with detailed design should be transferred to the contractor.

Contractor's designed portions (CDPs)

As systems and components become more technologically advanced, it is vital to consider whether members of the design team are the most suitable designers to take responsibility for these areas of the design. This requires identifying packages of work where the detailed design should be carried out by those with the greatest understanding of the systems involved – more often than not this will be the contractor and their subcontractors or suppliers. This decision will affect the scopes of services of both the design team and the contractor, which is why this issue must be considered earlier rather than later. The most common packages that are generally considered suitable for contractor design are substructure, superstructure, facades and mechanical, electrical and plant (MEP) packages.

The decision to procure CDPs will affect the level of detail in the information provided by the design team at Stage 4. A package where the contractor takes responsibility for the design will constitute design intent only by the design team, which means that the design information (both drawings and specifications) is developed to a level of detail that safeguards the appearance and performance of a particular component or system within the building. The specification is likely to avoid proprietary description, which is generally the most specific form of specification (ie the least room for manoeuvre by the contractor and the maximum responsibility taken by the designer). The responsibilities in respect of scope for each member of the design team, including the contractor, will have to be defined within the Design Responsibility Matrix, which is discussed later in the chapter.

Executive designers

It is increasingly common for larger, more complex projects to warrant a different approach in the design strategy. One such approach is to engage the services of an executive designer to take on the responsibilities associated with the detailed delivery of a design. Reasons for considering this option can vary and some are summarised as follows:

I the concept designer has proven design creativity but no track record in delivery of a detailed design

I the executive designer has a greater ability to resource the project with appropriate expertise in design delivery

I in the case of overseas projects, the executive designer is based locally and understands the specifics of local code compliance, construction capabilities, specification and even local culture

I the executive designer's fees are more competitive.

There are many issues that influence the decision to involve an executive designer (such as consistency, quality, local knowledge, efficiency and flexibility) and these should be considered at the outset before this route is pursued.

Production consultants

A variation on the appointment of an executive designer is the option to outsource the resources required for the detailed design. Production houses provide these resources to assist in the production of the necessary contract information. This option may be attractive to some designers who do not have the resources in-house but want to retain responsibility and control over the detailed design.

Each design strategy has numerous variables, such as the point at which responsibility is transferred, level of design responsibility and roles relating to quality monitoring and coordination.

Understanding the design strategy is important for the client as there are various instances where certain areas of scope will be taken on by a specialist subcontractor outside of the design team, as it is a waste of designers' resources and time to develop the design of systems that may or may not be used. The design team's fee agreements should state a position on design strategy to reassure the client that they are not paying twice for the same scope of work.

A common contention relates to the associated design costs of CDPs. The motive for allocating CDPs should not just relate to the transfer of design risk but should also encourage a collective understanding of who is most appropriate in terms of expertise and experience to assume the responsibility for the design. The design team needs to judge how far to take their design before handing over its completion to specialists but, despite the apparent reduction in scope, the design team takes on additional services in the liaison, review and eventual approval of shop drawings which will often offset any saving achieved by the reduced level of detail in the design information.

Who needs to be in the project team?

For larger projects there are many parties in the project team as well as numerous third party stakeholders and it is essential that the project lead identifies, notifies and communicates the appropriate level of commitment required to ensure that each party's inputs are coordinated and received in a timely manner. Initially, this will involve determining each party's level of authority to make sure they understand how they fit into the bigger picture in the definition of the Initial Project Brief. To assist in obtaining a consensus on the roles of the various project team members at every stage of the RIBA Plan of Work, the project lead should complete a Project Roles Table (figure 1.1).

The Project Roles Table is often not properly understood on larger projects where your day–to–day client contact may not have the authority to make the decisions necessary to progress the work. It is therefore prudent to address this sensitive issue as early as possible so the necessary steps in obtaining client approvals during the design stages can be properly planned into the process and included in the Project Execution Plan.

More important than any other point in the design process is the ability to obtain an appropriate level of client and third party input during the Preparation and Brief stage of the project. This is the point when the

	0 Strategic Definition	1 Preparation and Brief	2 Concept Design	3 Developed Design
Client				
Client adviser				
Project lead				
Lead designer				
Construction lead				
Architect				
Civil and structural engineer				
Building services engineer				
Cost consultant				
Contract administrator				
Health and safety adviser				
Access consultant				
Acoustic consultant				
Archaeologist				

Figure 1.1   Project Roles Table

client requirements are defined and validated, essentially formulating the 'question' to which the design team will respond during the design stages. If you don't know the question, you'll never provide the correct answer.

The project lead will therefore have to map out the process by which contributions are to be obtained and validated to avoid conflicting requirements that relate more to the individuals' departmental agendas than those of an integrated client body.

The design team for a larger project should be able to respond to the inputs and requirements of the client and will therefore often involve all core disciplines and appropriate specialists to minimise the iterations during the following design stages.

The health and safety adviser should be appointed as early as possible, and before any initial design work, which includes Feasibility Studies.

For smaller projects it is equally important to identify the roles and responsibilities of all concerned, although there will be fewer participants in the process. This information can then be extracted and arranged into a contractual tree to ensure that all design team members understand their working relationships (figure 1.2).

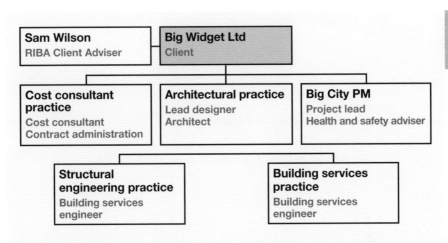

Figure 1.2   *Contractual Tree diagram*

Late appointment of design team members

It is particularly important for the project lead to identify all appointments necessary to carry out the works. Some clients will not want to invest in a complete design team at such an early stage, especially if their objective is to obtain a planning consent rather than see the project through to tender and construction. Some design team members will be more essential than others in this early part of the process so it is important to understand the specialist input required, the risks of not receiving that input and whether the design can accommodate that input during a later stage with minimal impact.

Reactive consultants vs proactive input

The design process needs to be mapped out by the project lead in a way that encourages the optimum input from the design team. There is a increasing trend for certain design team members to wait for the lead designer to develop their design to a point of resolution and fixity that minimises the number of iterations required by those other members of the design team. This may not result in the most effective or efficient solution and the project lead must establish with each member of the design team how they will proactively contribute to the developing design rather than respond to it.

Professional services contract

In order to engage the participation of the appropriate consultants it is necessary to consider the appointments strategy. This can take the form of a simple letter of intent or, more advisably, commence the formal appointment process to obtain the proper level of commitment from all involved. The key components of the professional service contracts are:

I Schedule of Services
I Design Responsibility Matrix
I Information Exchanges
I terms and conditions
I agreed fee proposals
I key personnel
I Project Programme.

Schedule of Services

The Schedule of Services will vary for each design team member and will be informed by the scale and complexity of the project. However, it is the role of the project lead to collate and review the submitted schedules from each consultant and be comfortable that the Schedules of Services required to successfully deliver the project are complete and coordinated.

Standard schedules

Most architectural practices have a tried and tested standard Schedule of Services but, to ensure that this covers the appropriate level of involvement, it is worth referencing the *Small Project Services Schedule 2013* (RIBA Plan of Work 2013 compatible version) if the project is small and relatively simple and the *Standard Agreement 2010 Schedules (2012 revision)* – which is RIBA Plan of Work 2013 compatible – if the project is larger and requires a greater level of accountability.

It is particularly important that the individual design team member's schedules are coordinated to avoid duplication and omissions in the services to be provided. This is commonly achieved by outlining the duties of each consultant and coordinating them by completing a Design Responsibility Matrix.

Design Responsibility Matrix

The Design Responsibility Matrix (figure 1.3) is a tool used by the project lead and the design team to coordinate the design responsibilities of multiple design team members, and also clarifies the extent of contractor's designed portions, allowing the design team to understand the level of information to be provided at Stage 4. It works by identifying a comprehensive list of building elements in the rows of the table. The consultant disciplines are then added to the column headings of the table. The intersection of boxes that correlate to both the element and the consultant are occupied with one of the following symbols that relate to the level of responsibility required of each consultant for each duty:

P   primary responsibility
S   secondary responsibility
A   advisory.

Once completed, it will be necessary to obtain approval from all the parties identified in the Design Responsibility Matrix to avoid potential conflicts at a later stage in the project.

A full explanation of the function of the Design Responsibility Matrix can be found in *Assembling a Collaborative Project Team* (chapter 7, page 75) by Dale Sinclair (RIBA Publishing, 2013).

Information Exchanges

The purpose of identifying the content of the Information Exchanges is to make sure that each member of the project team can properly plan their resources and therefore be confident that their fee proposal provides the appropriate level of commitment needed to complete the activities necessary to deliver the design to meet the client's expectations. Again, the collation of the stage Information Exchanges is the responsibility of the project lead, in consultation with the lead designer. The information is commonly made up of sketches, drawings, reports, specifications, schedules, calculations, models (3D and solid) and renderings. These should be listed for each stage for each project team member and be included in the professional services contracts at the earliest opportunity.

Aspect of design		2 - Concept Design			3 - Developed Design		
Classification	Title	Design responsibility	Level of design	Information Exchange	Design responsibility	Level of design	Information Exchange
15-05	Substructure						
15-05-65	Piling						
15-65-75	Insitu concrete frame						
15-65-75	Post tensioned concrete frame						
15-65-75	Precast concrete frame						
15-65-75	Steel frame including secondary steel						
20-10-20	Suspended ceilings						
20-15-05	Hard landscaping						
20-25-75	Roof lights						
20-50-30	Flat roof systems						
20-50-50	Metal sheet roof systems						
20-55	Carpets and other floor finishes						
20-55-15	Screeds						
20-55-35	Internal floor tiling						
20-55-70	Raised access floors						
20-55-95	Timber flooring						

Figure 1.3 Extract from a Design Responsibility Matrix

The level of design column attempts to clarify what is expected in terms of drawing scale, level of detail and therefore resolution.

For further information related to the definition of the levels of design refer to the *Level of Development Specification*, version: 2013, prepared by the BIMForum (http://bimforum.org).

Terms and conditions

The terms and conditions outline a catalogue of clauses that are commonly written up by the client's legal advisers and, upon signature, will be contractually binding. They are intended to define the rules by which the client wishes to engage the consultants and it is critical that each consultant reviews these to make sure that they are not committing themselves to a contract that cannot be honoured or tolerated. The project lead will act as the mediator by liaising with all consultants to obtain a collective 'buy-in' but, ultimately, each party must seek legal advice to make sure they are comfortable with all the terms and conditions before they sign. The subject matter covered varies again depending on the level of accountability sought by a client – however, it should not be more onerous than is appropriate to the scale and complexity of the project otherwise it becomes a potential obstacle to the smooth running of the contract. Common clauses to expect are:

I applicable law
I liability and insurances
I warranties
I consultants' obligations
I communications and approvals
I dispute resolution
I health and safety statements
I confidentiality and intellectual property
I payment terms
I termination procedures
I penalty conditions.

Agreed fee proposals

The fee proposal is a key part of the professional services contract and the project lead will usually ensure that the approach by all design team members is consistent with both the expectations of the client and the needs of the project. The fee proposals need to cross refer to the Initial Project Brief, Project Programme, the Design Responsibility Matrix and the professional services contract itself. It is sensible for each project team member to base their fee on a clear understanding of the resources that will be needed over the period to complete the activities required of them and it is increasingly common to include such a resource assessment within the fee proposal.

Fees for small projects

On smaller projects it is common to base the fee on a percentage of the construction costs alone, although market forces and overzealous clients could squeeze this figure below acceptable levels, leaving the design team with little confidence that the fee will satisfy the resourcing needs of the project. It could therefore be beneficial to negotiations on the fee to include the resource profile to demonstrate the basis of the fee calculation.

Key personnel

Including the CVs of key personnel is a common requirement of most professional services contracts, especially where a project has been 'won' on the basis that the client was particularly impressed by personnel in attendance at the interview. The information included within the CVs should be limited to data relevant to the needs of the project.

Project Programme

The professional services contract will need to incorporate a Project Programme, even if it is aspirational at this stage. This will link with the fee and resource proposals and provides the design team member and the client with an agreed timeframe. The Project Programme should contain, as a minimum, the design stages outlined in the RIBA Plan of Work 2013 including time frames, a period for procurement based on early assumptions of the most appropriate route, the anticipated Construction Programme, a period for handover and commissioning and a target completion date. The Project Programme is discussed in more detail on pages 54–7.

The Initial Project Brief

It is important for the project lead to ascertain whether the Core Objectives of the previous stage have been met prior to commencing the next stage. Efficient progress will be dependent on each stage being properly resolved and documented to be able to act as a point of reference for the follow-on activities.

The process of defining and testing the feasibility of an Initial Project Brief is not a linear one and each requirement will need to be tested for viability until there is a satisfactory balance between all conflicting objectives. This has historically, and rather simplistically, been described as the cost, time and quality triangle or, more appropriately in terms of the demands on the design team, the impossible Escher triangle of wanting all three – cheap, fast and excellent. Only two out of the three requirements can be properly delivered, hence the necessity to collaborate to achieve an acceptable balance between the three.

The fourth variable is, of course, 'content' or 'scope', although this is commonly associated with 'quality'. Nevertheless, if the team is struggling to balance the three requirements then reducing the 'content' must be recognised as a valid option.

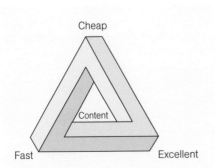

Figure 1.4   Getting the balance right

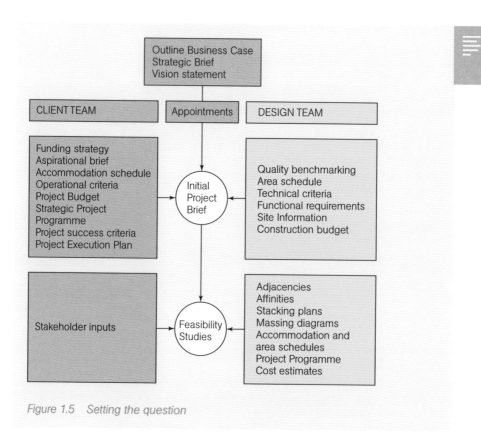

Figure 1.5 *Setting the question*

In general terms, the Initial Project Brief needs to set the question and provide sufficient direction to the design team so that the following design process can be executed without having to revisit fundamental requirements that affect the efficient progression of a Concept Design response. Figure 1.5 explains the sequence and common content of the Initial Project Brief and the Feasibility Studies that validate it.

The key components of an Initial Project Brief for all members of the design team will be determined by the project lead and the client, although many non-expert clients will be unaware of what should be decided at this stage of the process.

Assumptions in lieu of hard data

If, during the briefing stage, there is a lack of available information or insufficient expertise in the client team to provide adequate direction to the design team on essential aspects of core operational and functional elements of the Initial Project Brief, then it may be necessary for the design team to supplement the information by making assumptions based on experience and precedent building studies. If this is the case, these assumptions should be properly communicated by the project lead to the client and approval obtained before responding to the need in the following design stage.

For larger projects more information needs to be captured but the basic premise applies to smaller projects and the key components will fall under the following headings:

I Project Objectives and/or Project Outcomes
I operational strategies
I functional requirements
I technical requirements
I spatial criteria.

Project Objectives and Project Outcomes

This section of the Initial Project Brief provides the opportunity for the client to record at the earliest opportunity everything that they consider precious about their organisation, their vision and the project need that was outlined at a high level in the Strategic Brief during Stage 0. This section must be authored by the client to avoid potential misinterpretation as the client knows their business better than anyone.

Sustainability Aspirations discussed and agreed during Stage 0 should be developed further and agreed as part of the Initial Project Brief at Stage 1, since early consideration of the extent of sustainable and integrated design alongside the method of measurement (BREEAM/LEED etc.) could have a significant impact on cost and process.

In the previous stage the client will have worked through their Strategic Brief and Business Case, which could be a series of complex commercial and market calculations for a larger, more complex project or a simple demonstration that the funding is in place for a smaller and more straightforward project. Either way, the Project Objectives recorded in the Initial Project Brief will be the springboard that ensures everything that follows has a point of reference to which the design response can be compared. Aside from reinforcing the client vision, the Project Objectives will also include high-level assessments of both the Project Budget and the Project Programme, which will be properly tested by the design team during the Feasibility Studies and subsequently validated.

It is highly recommended that the project lead instigates a quality benchmarking exercise to help support the Project Objectives. This will involve implementing precedent studies of several similar buildings to ascertain whether the quality achieved in the 'as-built' condition can be used as an example of the intended quality for the current project. This exercise can be used to benchmark the overall design quality, materiality, space standards and operational principles of tried and tested examples in a similar environment. It is usual for desktop studies to be carried out by the design team and, if appropriate, visits should be arranged to witness the buildings at first hand. The study is usually supplemented by a cost benchmarking exercise so that indicative comparison can be made at this early stage to assess suitability.

The desired outcomes for the project (for example, in the case of a school this might be an improvement in examination results) may include operational aspects and a mixture of subjective and objective criteria.

It may also be desirable to set out the quality aspects of a project. Like the project outcomes, the objectives may be made up from both subjective and objective features, although subjective features may require a design quality indicator (DQI) benchmark review during Stage 7.

Operational strategies

The operational strategies to some extent inform the accommodation schedule in that they define how the building(s) will be run.

Operational strategy for cleaning

Is it the intention to have a centralised cleaning store, smaller cleaning cupboards distributed throughout the building or to contract out cleaning to an external service provider that has no need to store cleaning materials?

Most operational aspects of the building will be considered by the client; however, for inexperienced clients, many questions will need to be raised by an experienced design team in establishing the need.

There are many such issues where a client may prefer to increase the operational budget rather than impact the capital expenditure over which they have control. There are many instances of project teams ignoring the value of increased capital expenditure to enhance specifications that could obtain financial recovery throughout the design life of a building by reducing the operational costs. This is predominantly because, in most cases, the capital budgets are ringfenced and inflexible, even when over a 30-year period the benefits of an increased capital spend can demonstrably result in year-on-year reductions in operating costs. The project lead should advise the client that the ability to transfer between their budgets should remain flexible until the advantages can be properly assessed during the briefing process.

Operational strategy for plant

More expensive building plant can yield operational efficiencies over cheaper equipment and more robust (and expensive) building materials will require less servicing over the life span of the building.

This does, of course, work both ways; if, for example, the Initial Project Brief requires a building to be constructed to Government Indemnity Standards (specific to the protection of highly insured or priceless content, such as the contents of a museum), an alternative to significant capital expenditure could be provided by temporary installations of higher grade plant or increased resources instead of costly electronic security measures within the infrastructure of the building. On a domestic scale, this could equally apply to proposing, as a alternative to the two spaces in the project brief, a single space with dual use thereby reducing the duplication of building components, services and finishes.

One of the common misconceptions often encountered when trying to define the components of an Initial Project Brief is the client's reluctance to commit, as they would prefer the building to be flexible. Flexibility needs definition, as much as any other aspect of the Initial Project Brief, as flexibility costs money, whether it is due to the inclusion of increased electrical outlets or more space to accommodate a variety of activities. This is not an area where the Initial Project Brief can remain silent; if flexibility is a key aspiration then it will generally result in an increase in area, specification and, ultimately, costs.

Functional requirements

It is important to differentiate between functional requirements and operational strategies – they sound similar but the functional aspects of an Initial Project Brief are helping to define the space standards rather than the accommodation or specification. This provides justification for the extent of the space outlined in the accommodation schedule by looking in more detail at what the space will be used for and how it is to be used. This justification is particularly important to have in place to counter potential pressure to reduce costs, which will inevitably target area or volume reductions in the first instance. It is the functional brief that will defend the scheduled areas from 'easy' savings later in the process when it may not be clear what has informed the choice of area of a particular room in the first instance.

Technical requirements

The technical requirements have the potential to inform many aspects of the Initial Project Brief including aspirational, operational and spatial and this section is probably more demanding on specialist consultant input than any other. Technical requirements relate to the performance of the space, equipment or materials that will be used in the building. They can have a huge impact on both cost and time and, if incorrectly assessed, will undoubtedly have an impact on the resultant quality of the building.

It is in this section of the Initial Project Brief that the desired comfort levels are stated (temperature, humidity, acoustic insulation, dryness etc.)

and also quality definitions (such as resilience, design life, service life etc.) are outlined at an early stage to steer the design team towards the appropriate design response. If this is left until later in the process then much time can be wasted on investigating decisions that could affect cost and quality when these issues should have been reviewed during the Feasibility Studies. It stands to reason that anything that has the potential to significantly affect the cost or quality of the building ought to have been raised as an issue that impacts the feasibility of the Initial Project Brief rather than something that is 'optioneered' during the design process.

Design life vs service life

During the definition of technical criteria in the briefing period, it is advisable to understand the implications of capital expenditure on life cycle costs. The design life defines how long irreplaceable components of the building are expected by their designers to work within their specified parameters: in other words, the life expectancy of the component. The service life of secondary components (the point at which replacement is required) has a direct relationship with the design life of primary components and is factored into the running costs of a building. Components with shorter service lives cost less at the outset but will increase the operational costs of the building. Achieving the appropriate balance requires discussion with the client during the briefing period so that agreement can be reached.

Inappropriate standards

Standards impact the ability to balance the brief in the same way as other components of the Initial Project Brief. They set out prescriptive requirements for quality that affect specification and workmanship that may not be achievable in certain geographical locations or using the skills of the tier of contractor being considered for the project. Extra costs could be introduced into tenders where the interpretation of onerous standards is misunderstood or even unknown. The standards referred to should be made to align with both the Project Budget and the ability of contractors to meet them.

CIBSE Guide A: Environmental design, 7th edition, table 1.1 recommendations for internal design conditions should be used as base principles of design. A non-exhaustive summary of these conditions is given in table 1.1:

Table 1.1   Examples of technical criteria

DWELLINGS	WINTER TEMP (°C)	SUMMER TEMP (°C)	AIR SUPPLY RATE (L/S PER PERSON)	MAINTAINED ILLUMINANCE (LUX)	NOISE RATING (NR VALUE)
Bathrooms	20–22	–	15	150	–
Bedrooms	17–19	Comfort cooling	0.4–1 ACH	100	25
Halls/stairs etc.	19–24	Comfort cooling	–	100	–
Kitchen	17–19	Comfort cooling	60	150–300	40–45
Living rooms	22–23	Comfort cooling	0.4–1 ACH	50–300	30
Toilets	19–21	–	>5 ACH	100	–
Common areas	TBA	Comfort cooling	TBA	TBA	TBA
Garages		–			
Parking	–	–	6 ACH	75/300	55
Servicing	16–19	–		300/500	45–50

ACH = air changes per hour

CIBSE guidance

For further information on the available guidance and codes published by CIBSE visit their website at www.cibse.org/

Spatial criteria

The spatial criteria are the product of almost all other components of the Initial Project Brief and will therefore be subject to much iteration in achieving the correct balance between cost and quality. Spatial refers not only to area but also to volume, which will have been defined as part of the functional requirements. The spatial criteria are generally expressed as an area schedule that has volume accounted for by the inclusion of room heights. At this stage in the process an area schedule that includes volumetric data will be critical in reconciling square metre rates in order to both establish and test the high-level Project Budget.

Setting up Post-occupancy Evaluation criteria

In most instances, design teams end their involvement with a building at completion of the construction works. The performance of the building beyond that date historically has rarely been reviewed against the design parameters – this approach is now changing and the RIBA Plan of Work 2013 recognises the need to encourage a more proactive approach in supporting the client during the handover process.

Every project provides a client with a platform to change and improve practices and introduce new and improved working methods or, in the case of domestic projects, simply to change the way they lead their lives. It provides organisations with the opportunity to change, or indeed support a changing culture. However, it is important to review and evaluate this transition post occupancy to ensure that the desired change and improvement has been achieved.

There is a range of measures that will help the client to familiarise themselves with the new building. The Post-occupancy Evaluation process is a comprehensive review of the building in operational and user terms, which seeks to identify any shortfalls in expectations or, indeed, any areas for improvement. It is therefore necessary to identify at the outset the criteria by which the building's performance can be measured, this will be either relative to the emerging design criteria or the performance/satisfaction rating of an existing facility.

This process should therefore be adopted as a way of reducing unnecessary changes to completed schemes, saving clients' money and management time. As Post-occupancy Evaluations are becoming

Post-occupancy questions

What questions need to be asked in Post-occupancy Evaluations?
- Does the building perform in accordance with the design criteria?
- Does it still address the users' needs?
- What issues require immediate attention?
- How effective was the design process from inception to completion?
- What lessons can be learned for future projects?

increasingly more commonplace, utilising client feedback to better inform future projects should become the norm. The content of Post-occupancy Evaluations should be tailored to the specific purpose of the buildings to make sure that they address the peculiarities of particular uses.

Project Budget

At Stage 1 the Project Budget will usually be based on a square metre rate ($£/m^2$) due to the obvious lack of design information to price. Metre rates are therefore based on the cost consultant's experience or publicly available data relating to similar recently completed projects. Due to commercial sensitivity this data can be difficult to obtain for all building typologies but for smaller projects, such as one-off houses, the information is readily available and relatively reliable. Metre rates are generally built up by a more detailed understanding of key component rates, such as facade rates, MEP rates and proven rates for interior finishes. Adjustments will need to be made in rates obtained from precedent studies to account for both location and year-on-year inflation if the building was completed some time ago.

It is important for the project lead to understand the difference between Project Budget and construction budget. Generally, the Project Budget includes all direct costs to the client in relation to the project. These are not the costs that the design team will use for fee benchmarking purposes and many of the costs are invisible to the design team as they do not relate to the construction budget for the building. The Project Budget should not be confused with a cost estimate. A Project Budget will include the total of the cost estimate, and will also include what are known as 'soft costs'. These soft costs will be specifically excluded from the cost estimate and will typically include land acquisition, architectural and design fees, movable furniture and equipment, building permits and fees, and fire and all risks insurance.

The Project Budget will also include non-construction related costs, such as fundraising and moving costs. Project costs can be as much as 30–40% higher than the construction budget, so it is important for the project lead to make the client fully aware that their financial commitment to the project does not stop at how much it costs to build.

Another key responsibility for the project lead is to ensure that the client's Business Case includes a funding strategy for the project. This could be straightforward in smaller projects but in larger projects, especially

Project Budget vs construction budget

Project Budget
- project contingencies
- client advisory fees
- inflation
- legal fees
- insurances
- professional fees
- design contingency
- statutory fees
- site investigations
- IT and audio/visual equipment
- construction budget
- fixtures, fitting and equipment
- relocation/removals costs
- freestanding fire equipment

Construction budget
- main contract works
- preliminaries
- contractor's overheads
- contractor's profit
- fit-out
- landscaping
- construction risk allowance
- in-house costs and expenses (including all central support services, administration, overheads etc.)
- wayleaves and compensation
- demolition and diversion of existing facilities
- insurances.

public sector projects, it can impact the Project Programme as funding gateways will need to be adhered to.

Government procured projects have stringent requirements in terms of completion of specific information exchanges, often involving approvals at several stages during the design process before they can secure funding. The funding can also emanate from various different sources, which complicates the process further.

The principles of cost management are an important aspect for the project lead to set out correctly at this stage in order to define and monitor the costs for the duration of the project. All costs, whether project or construction, should be accounted for and appropriate budgets set aside to meet the Project Objectives for continuing control throughout the design period.

The cost consultant is a key member of the design team and in any project structure should provide continuous advice and management of the costs rather than cost reporting following interim Information Exchanges. Continuous review of the design development by regular attendance at workshops will provide early warnings of cost overruns that can be addressed as part of the iterative process rather than becoming an unwelcome distraction if they arise from review at formal Information Exchanges. The project lead must be open and honest with the client and communicate issues early enough for the client to participate in prioritising their aspirations and objectives. Treating the client as part of the design team will result in a collaborative approach with reduced iteration and abortive work.

The client is ultimately responsible for balancing the costs according to their priorities and will certainly not thank the design team for being furtive about communicating potential cost overruns.

It is usual for the client to identify project contingencies in case of unpredictable issues, such as a change in brief or specification, changes in statutory compliance, tax etc. These contingencies are usually separated out, with the client being responsible for the expenditure of some and the project lead having delegated responsibility for the utilisation of others. Typical contingencies are:

Project contingencies

Project contingency	Typically controlled by the client to cover high-level events, such as a change in legislation or programme
Design contingency	Typically controlled by the project lead (in consultation with the lead designer) to cover events such as a change in the brief or beneficial design development
Construction contingency	Typically controlled by the contract administrator to cover events such as unforeseen site conditions

The level of contingency will vary according to the scale and complexity of the project, and the cumulative total could be up to 15% of the value of the project, depending on the anticipated level of risk and certainty. The contingency allowances will generally reduce with the reduction in risk as the level of design certainty increases as the design progresses.

Proper definition of contingencies

As discussed earlier in this chapter, it is essential that the client, the project lead and the design team understand the circumstances that trigger the utilisation of contingencies. They are often relied upon in cases where the balance of aspiration, need and budget have not been properly defined during the briefing process when they should in fact be used solely for the purpose of covering unforeseen events that occur during the development of the project.

Measures essential to maintaining expenditure within the Project Budget include the following:

I *Accurate and comprehensive cost estimate*, with no scope gaps or duplication.

I *Adequate contingencies*, informed by an understanding of financial risk. Wherever possible, risks should be quantified to ensure that contingency allowances are informed by considered opinion, rather than an arbitrary rule of thumb.

I *Budgetary control during the design phase* – each design stage gateway will be supported by a report which reconciles the proposed design to a contemporaneous cost plan and an updated risk register.

I *Effective and accurate cost reporting*, covering all cost headings and encapsulated in a total expenditure forecast. This document will allow the project lead to agree the client's cost centres and establish budget ownership. The project lead will rely on the expert advice of the cost consultant, and challenge the design team to improve efficiency.

I *Adoption of an appropriate procurement strategy* – this will be based on an examination of all the options available to the project and an analysis of the effects of each in terms of cost security, compliance with the relevant regulations and the transfer of financial risk (see page 57).

I *Diligent application of a robust Change Control Procedure* – it will be necessary for the project lead to devise and operate a bespoke change management process which will establish a sponsor for any proposed change and identify a justification to demonstrate the benefit to be derived from it.

I *A 'right first time' culture*, avoiding wasted resources and unnecessary cost.

Budget vs quality mismatch

The success of any project is reliant on achieving a match between the quality aspirations and the budget at the outset. If this is resolved during the feasibility stage then the following design stages can be progressed in an efficient manner with minimal iterations and abortive work.

Area vs volume

Discussed in earlier sections, volume has as much of an implication on cost as area, so it is vital that the volumetric data is also incorporated into the Initial Project Brief.

Methods of measurement

It must be understood from the outset which methods will be applied in the measurement of area, performance and progress. All are open to interpretation and, to ensure that expectations are aligned at the start of a project, there must be a discussion on which methods will be utilised.

Inflation

With projects of significant duration, inflation needs to be factored into the Project Budget to accommodate predicted increases in contractors' tenders. Inflation that will impact mainly on the construction budget will nevertheless be incorporated into the overall Project Budget.

Project Programme

The Project Programme is a critical tool in the management of any project and it is the responsibility of the project lead to produce and maintain the Project Programme at all stages of the project. Although the Project Programme will be fixed, there will undoubtedly be a need to revisit it, either to incorporate the effect of change or in response to other, unforeseen delays. At the commencement of the project, the Project Programme should include, as a minimum, the following activities:

Components of the Project Programme

- A period for Stage 0, Strategic Definition
- A period for Stage 1, Preparation and Brief
- The design strategy (including the milestones indicated in the RIBA Plan of Work 2013 Stages 2–4 as appropriate)
- Indicative statutory approvals strategy
- Indicative procurement strategy
- Construction period – Stage 5
- Fit-out period
- Handover and Close Out period – Stage 6
- Project completion
- In Use support activities – Stage 7

There are many different formats that a Project Programme can use: on larger projects the most common format is a Gantt chart, with activities intelligently linked to allow the programme to be interrogated and updated with ease (figure 1.6). This format, however, is not easy on the eye and therefore not always best suited to communicate the design process within a stage.

Other than mapping out the activities and the timeframe for all participants, the Project Programme should also be set out in such a way that progress can be properly monitored.

In support of the Project Programme, and at each stage of the design, the project lead will need to make sure that the lead designer has prepared a Design Programme that supports the Project Programme and provides a greater level of detail to explain how the design team is to progress the design. Ideally, the Design Programme should be prepared in advance of the stage to which it applies, which means that during Stage 1 Preparation and Brief the lead designer should prepare the Design Programme for Stage 2 Concept Design. For the purposes of this guide the principles of the Design Programme will be explained in the next chapter.

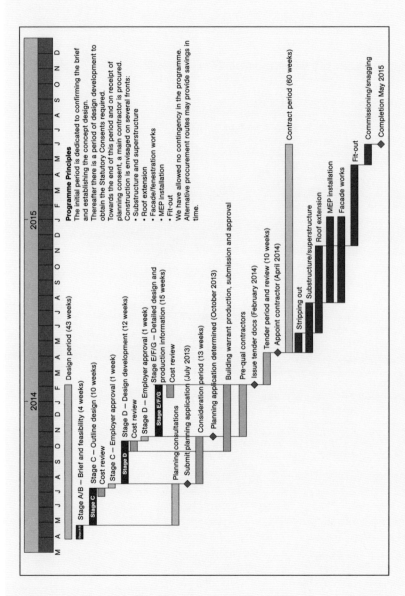

Figure 1.6   Example of simplified Project Programme

Unrealistic timescales

There are ways of speeding up the design and delivery process, such as employing more aggressive procurement strategies with earlier transfer of risk to the contractor and increased use of contractor's designed portions. However, the project lead will need to communicate the implications of these options on quality and obtain the client's agreement.

Procurement

Procurement of construction is a big topic and one which requires discussion rather than presentation of preconceived ideas of which route is appropriate. However, to give a taste of how the project lead would come to the best decision, some key decision-making criteria and a diagram showing the options with their characteristics/profiles are set out here.

Procurement vs contract

There is a common misunderstanding between procurement strategy and contract type; in simple terms, the procurement strategy dictates the method by which the contractor's services and the construction elements of the building are bought whereas the contract type is a legally binding arrangement that defines the responsibilities between the contractor and the client.

The appropriate approach to procurement is to always start by understanding the client's objectives in relation to risk, time, cost, quality and flexibility to change. There is no definitive 'right or wrong' procurement strategy that can be applied to all schemes; the project lead will need to set the scene during briefing and design development, as the relationship is built with the client team.

The key issues associated with the development of the optimum procurement strategy are as follows:

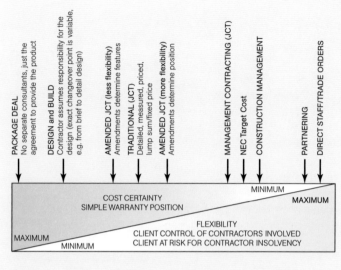

Figure 1.7   Procurement considerations

I   definition of the point at which cost certainty is required
I   assessment of the risk burden and agreement of where it should lie
I   definition of the acceptable cost of achieving risk transfer
I   consideration of the degree of control over the design that is required
I   validation of the procurement timeline.

These issues will need to be carefully discussed with the key contributors to the procurement strategy and, using the conclusions drawn from Risk Assessment workshops, risk management exercises and discussions with the client, cost consultant and other relevant key third parties, it will be necessary to agree where the burden of risk should lie.

The decision regarding whether the risk should be shared or borne by one particular party will greatly influence the proposed procurement route.

The project lead should undertake an in-depth analysis to evaluate the respective weighting associated with time, cost and quality to support the evaluation of tenders.

The proposed procurement strategy will be developed by the project lead and submitted to the client for approval. This document will include:

I the detailed process to be adopted
I the aims to be achieved
I a definition of any residual risks which remain with the client
I the agreed basis of the evaluation process
I the activity schedules and linked programme.

The provision of a formal procurement strategy document ensures that all parties clearly understand the process and what it is meant to achieve.

Common building contracts

A standard form of building contract is a binding agreement between the client (the employer) and the contractor who is responsible for carrying out the construction work. It will include full details of the costs, labour, materials and services as well as the contract plans, specifications, drawings and a Construction Programme. The construction work to be executed, including the cost and programme, must comply with the contract.

Common building contracts

JCT (the Joint Contracts Tribunal)

The JCT is a well-known suite of contracts that is widely used in the construction industry and is generally clearly understood by all associated with building projects (contractors, design teams and clients). The longevity of the form's use promotes this deep level of understanding, which in turn is enhanced by extensive case law relating to JCT projects. It must, however, be noted that JCT forms are often regarded as legally biased due to the way in which causation is drafted. At times, this can lead to difficulties with onsite interpretation, which in turn causes problems with overall administration (this issue, however, was addressed in part in 2005 editions, in which the terminology used was simplified). The JCT form of contract can be used in varying formats to suit the particular procurement route chosen and this is obviously a key benefit during the earlier stages of a project where this decision has yet to be made.

The JCT is regarded by many as slightly employer biased. At times this does not, in fact, benefit a client as in many instances they

Common building contracts (*continued*)

are not best placed to deal with the risks imposed on them. As a result this often leads to extensive amendments to the drafting of the clauses that in turn take away an element of the clarity that the contract possesses in its unamended form.

On a final note, JCT forms are, by their nature, more adversarial than other contract alternatives. This can either lead to a highly contentious situation or, conversely, can be operated in a much less confrontational manner, as long as all parties commit to resolving their differences quickly and constructively.

NEC (New Engineering Contract)

Like the JCT this contract can be adapted to suit any specific procurement route by use of core and secondary clauses that form the overall suite of documentation. This enables a project to 'mix and match' contractual forms from the overall suite of documentation, reducing the need to amend causation to make the contract specific.

The NEC is also drafted in simpler language than the JCT alternative. Experience has shown this to be both beneficial and problematic. While administration of the contract is comparatively easier at site level, the terminology used is often open to interpretation and can be too easily 'massaged' to benefit the party with a specific axe to grind.

Use of the NEC undoubtedly promotes a culture of proactive management of a project due to the dual responsibility of the project lead and the contractor to proactively advise and work together to resolve issues as and when they arise. However, and of crucial importance, for this form to work all parties associated with the project need to have experience of how to manage this form of contract, which contains provisions that are quite specific to the NEC (such as early warning notices, provisions of compensation events and management of the risk register). Appointment of a design team which is not familiar with the form can require negotiation of a steep learning curve which, if not carefully managed, can lead to programme delays.

PPC2000 (Public Procurement Contract)

Partnering contracts were developed to reduce the adversarial element in contracts and to achieve a greater

Common building contracts (*continued*)

level of cooperation. They involve creating an environment
of trust between the contracting parties through transparent
communications, information sharing and working collaboratively
towards a common objective. The partnering relationship
is crystallised in a charter and in the spirit of genuine trust.
Partnering does not replace the traditional contract, which legally
binds the parties in the transaction; rather, it is additional to it
and operates as a process requiring a positive mindset. If people
enter into an agreement where the underlying premise is trust
and openness, then there will be no need to refer to the formal
contract.

One type of partnering contract is the PPC2000. This type of
partnering contract was created to serve the needs of people
who want to adopt a more sophisticated approach to project
procurement. Part of the PPC2000 is a condition that states that
the involved parties will talk among themselves and discuss
the outline of the project. In doing this they need, first, to agree
a mutual set of objectives and then determine how they can
achieve them. The strength of PPC2000 is its desire to boost
the communication between members of the construction team
and other parities. PPC2000 cannot offer the solution for all
the challenges to be faced during the execution of a Building
Contract, as human nature is not a constant.

FIDIC (Fédération Internationale des Ingénieurs-Conseils)

More commonly known as 'the International Federation of
Consulting Engineers', FIDIC's Contracts Committee has
developed several standard forms of contract for both civil
engineering and building projects located overseas. It is best
known for its range of standard conditions of contract for the
construction, plant and design industries, which are the most
widely used forms of contract internationally. The purpose of
these standard forms is to define the contractual relationships
and identify and allocate risks between the contractor and the
client. They are generally considered as contracts that fairly
allocate risks to those parties who are best able to accept and
mitigate them.

The forms of contract are drafted for use on a wide range of
project types and are differentiated by the colour of their covers.

Common building contracts (*continued*)

The choice of form depends on the type of project being contemplated. In summary:

- straightforward, quick or cheap project – Green Book
- employer-appointed design team (traditional project) – Red Book
- employer-appointed design team (multilateral development banks providing finance) – Pink Book
- contractor design (traditional project) – Yellow Book
- energy procurement construction/turnkey project – Silver Book
- design, build, operate project – Gold Book

There is a key requirement under the Red and Yellow Books for the contractor to serve notice in respect of a claim for an extension of time or additional payment. The contractor must give notice of any intent to claim no later than 28 days after they become aware, or more importantly should have become aware, of an event. They must then submit their fully detailed claim within 42 days of becoming aware of the event – there is no entitlement to compensation if the contractor fails to comply with this requirement.

Choice of contract

Every contract has advantages and disadvantages depending on whose perspective they are viewed from. It should be remembered that the choice of contract alone will not create an environment of success; this will only come about by engendering a collaborative and fair culture throughout the negotiations and construction stage of a project. In an ideal world, the contract should be signed and kept in a drawer, only ever taken out to refer to process rather than behaviour. Every challenge that arises can be resolved by adopting a single team approach with open and honest interaction and a mutual understanding of what is best for the project rather than the individual.

Project Execution Plan (PEP)

In collaboration with the design team, the project lead will need to produce the Project Execution Plan, which describes the framework, strategies, practices and procedures for the execution and delivery of a project.

It is intended to:

I provide relevant, up-to-date information to the client, design team and other interested parties regarding how the project is being managed and delivered
I be a valuable orientation document for new recruits to the design team, ensuring consistency of delivery and quality.

The Project Execution Plan should outline Project Objectives based on the Strategic Brief, participants, responsibilities, procedures and control processes, often using sketches, charts and diagrams to communicate key messages. Any further reading material or relevant project information referred to in the document should be made available in the appendices, so that it can be hyperlinked to the live Project Execution Plan and updated when necessary.

Smaller thumbnail extracts of these appendices should appear in the text to enable the reader to recognise the document being referred to.

There will also be references to further background reading, such as the Business Case, Initial Project Brief or Building Information Modelling (BIM) protocols that cannot be attached as appendices due to size limitations. However, on all projects these documents form valuable background information supporting the Project Execution Plan.

The Project Execution Plan will be a live document, owned and kept up to date by the project lead with contributions from the design team and should be made available to all either via an online document collaboration tool or an FTP site. Revision to the document should occur as the need arises with a complete review every three months, or at a suitable interval dictated by the tempo of the project.

The typical contents of a Project Execution Plan will vary depending on the size and complexity of the project but the content highlighted in bold are common headings with more specific issues in italics being applicable to all sizes of project.

Typical Project Execution Plan contents

1.0 **Introduction**
2.0 **Key project information**
    2.1 Project particulars
    2.2 Vision and description
    2.3 Project team
    2.4 Phasing and timetable
    2.5 Budget summary
3.0 **Organisation and communication**
    3.1 Design team structure
    3.2 Roles and responsibilities
    3.3 Consultation and PR strategy
    3.4 Meeting strategy
    3.5 Reporting strategy
    3.6 Document control
    3.7 Communication
    3.8 Project directory
4.0 **Initial Project Brief**
5.0 **Stakeholder and third party engagement**
    5.1 Key stakeholders
    5.2 Planning and statutory approvals
6.0 **Quality**
7.0 **Time control**
    7.1 Employer key decisions
    7.2 Project Programme
    7.3 Design Programme
    7.4 Monitoring progress
8.0 **Risk and opportunity**
9.0 **Cost control**
    9.1 Cash flow
    9.2 Invoicing procedure
    9.3 Change control
    9.4 Requests for information (RFI procedure)
    9.5 Cost reporting
    9.6 Formal project reporting
10.0 **Procurement strategy**
11.0 **Legal and insurance**
    11.1 Consultant appointments
    11.2 Construction contracts
    11.3 Insurance
12.0 **Health and safety**
    12.1 Site regulations
13.0 **Testing, commissioning and handover**
14.0 **Recommended reading**

Site Information

During the data collection for the preparation of the Initial Project Brief there is an opportunity for the project lead to collect as much Site Information as possible on behalf of the client. This information will form the basis of validation activities during the Preparation and Brief stage.

The following are recommended surveys that will enhance the site information available to the design team during Stage 1 and the following design stages:

Site Information requirements

For new buildings

- legal boundaries
- dimensional and topographical survey
- tree condition surveys
- existing services and utilities survey
- soil investigations (will be required during Stage 2).

For existing buildings

- CCTV drainage integrity survey
- timber and damp survey – wet rot, dry rot, wood-boring insect infestation etc.
- contamination – lead (pipework or paint), horsehair plaster (anthrax spores, asbestos)
- asbestos – refurbishment asbestos survey (old type 3 survey)
- structural engineer's report (must be by an engineer familiar with historic assets).

Other surveys that may be required to help define the neighbourly aspects of the building:

- party wall
- rights of light.

Feasibility Studies

As mentioned in the introduction, the Feasibility Studies should not be used to commence conceptual design ideas, especially in respect of aesthetics, but need to focus on activities that demonstrate the viability of the Initial Project Brief. It is therefore essential that the project lead properly communicates these objectives to the lead designer to prevent them skipping forward to design – this tendency to embark on premature design must be avoided at all costs to ensure the aesthetic does not compromise the function.

This means taking the elements of the Initial Project Brief and testing them in diagrammatic form to understand where there are conflicts in satisfying the operational, spatial or functional requirements of the building. It is also an opportunity to prove whether the quality aspirations of the client can be met within the constraints of the Project Budget, the Project Programme and the site constraints. In order to achieve a prompt understanding of these criteria, a diagrammatic approach should be employed, which focuses purely on demonstrating workable principles rather than design solutions, addressing:

| affinities
| adjacencies
| 3D stacking plans
| massing diagrams
| accommodation and area schedules
| confirmation of the Project Programme
| confirmation of the Project Budget.

Preconceptions (pre-Concept Design)

The need to avoid preconceptions by the designers during Stage 1 cannot be overstressed. The main objective of the Feasibility Studies is to comprehensively test the requirements of the Initial Project Brief and establish the operational and functional priorities of the client. Adjustments should be made at a strategic level during this stage to avoid unnecessary iterations of the more detailed design proposals during the later design stages.

The Feasibility Studies are intended to ensure that the building works in terms of the client's need prior to proposing an aesthetic or conceptual idea into which the project parameters are shoehorned. The key aspects of a successful Feasibility Study will therefore concentrate on demonstrating that all the elements of the design can be achieved without compromising any aspect of the project parameters.

Affinities

Affinities studies are particular to larger projects and are essentially the identification of the relationships of the components of the project (ie building juxtaposition in a master plan or department groupings in a larger, more complex project).

Adjacencies

Adjacencies studies determine the optimum relationship between all elements of the accommodation schedule, how they are linked by the circulation strategy and how they are serviced by the distribution of cores and riser locations. These studies need to be considered in advance of any conceptual aesthetic thinking to ensure that the functional and operational aspects of the Initial Project Brief are the priority of the design team before committing to a style or form.

3D stacking plans

The stacking plans are a key aspect of the Feasibility Studies as they relate directly to the site-specific constraints of the project. The area of the site will determine how much area can be accommodated on each floor plate and therefore the number of floor plates required to satisfy the area aspirations of the Initial project Brief. Each floor plate is stacked on top of the other in isometric form and overlaid on the project site plan, providing a clearer understanding of the anticipated height and massing of the proposal.

Massing diagrams

Out of the stacking plan exercise comes the massing diagrams; the two studies will often go through several iterations in parallel until the optimum proposal is revealed. The massing diagrams help to identify the third dimension of volume to the accommodation schedule – an important influence on the Project Budget. For expediency, these are simple wire line diagrams and communicate no more than the potential 3D envelope of the building. Other site constraints will inform the potential massing, such as rights of light, urban context and planning guidance information.

Accommodation and area schedules

At this stage of the project, the area schedules have the greatest impact on the Project Budget, primarily because the budgets are established using square metre rates, as discussed earlier in this chapter. The rates will need to factor in the volumetric criteria associated with the areas so that floor-to-floor heights, atria and voids are factored into the costs. The accommodation and area schedules will have to keep pace with the other studies discussed above to ensure that the balance of aspiration and cost is maintained at all times.

Confirmation of the Project Programme

The studies detailed above will have to be tested against the Project Programme to determine the ability to deliver the design within the proposed timescales. This will require the project lead to ascertain the timescales required for each of the key components of the Project Programme and could also inform the preferred procurement route, depending on whether speed, cost or quality is the key driver of the Initial Project Brief. The ability to meet a programme requires an assessment by the majority of the design team with respect to the design and production periods required to respond to the scale and complexity of the brief. However, the project lead in consultation with the design team will be responsible for determining the timescales required for procurement and construction.

Confirmation of the Project Budget

As with all components of the Feasibility Studies, the Project Budget will need to be tested against the outputs of the Feasibility Studies in parallel. This will undoubtedly require a few iterations to make sure that the client's requirements can be properly studied, tested and confirmed as viable within the parameters laid out in the Initial Project Brief. Only when the client, the project lead and the design team are comfortable that all requirements are in balance and can be achieved is the design team ready to commence design activities in Stage 2 Concept Design.

Risk Assessments

As one of the potential support tasks identified in the RIBA Plan of Work 2013, risk is anything that can deflect a project from its planned course of action; it can be time, cost or quality related.

The project lead should adopt an approach to the management of risk that is proactive and simple but ensures that those aspects with the potential to adversely impact the project are properly identified and monitored. The project lead will need to focus on dealing with these aspects to minimise their probability and, should they occur, to ensure that the impact is controlled. The project can be exposed to different levels of risk, which need to be considered. There are those risks that sit outside the control of the design team – these are called project risks and could be anything from weather to war to issues affecting funding. The other category of risks are design risks – these could include variations from the Initial Project Brief, insufficient designer expertise or poor coordination.

The approach is two-staged; first to identify and analyse risks, and then to manage them in order to mitigate their effect.

Risk identification is an inclusive process which should involve all project participants. The focus should not just be on the immediate scope of the project but must consider those wider activities on which the project has a degree of dependency. Each identified risk will need to be reviewed to assess its potential probability of occurring and potential impact on the development of the project. At every stage of the project a risk workshop will have to be organised for the design team. An important aspect of risk

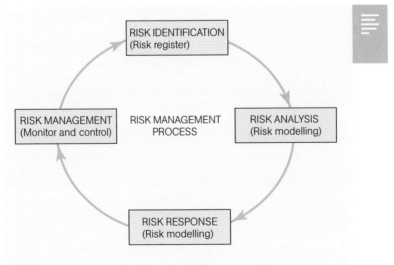

Figure 1.8   Risk management process

analysis is to ensure that each risk is allocated an owner, who is best placed to take action to mitigate the risk. This first stage culminates in the production of a risk register, which provides a control document for enabling the monitoring and management of the risks.

Risk management involves the regular monitoring of risks to establish any changes to the factors influencing whether the identified risks are worsening or reducing, and to highlight any new, developing risks. Risk management plans listing the actions to be undertaken to control the risks will be prepared by the project lead. A risk status report will need to be reviewed with the client each month.

As well as monitoring risks, it is equally important for the project lead to maintain a similarly disciplined approach to 'issues'; these are aspects which, if not adequately controlled, have the potential to develop into risks.

The project lead will play a significant part in identifying and assessing the risk and the following steps should be implemented to reduce residual risks:

How to reduce residual risks from the outset

– Aspirations must be realistic and achievable and the brief to support these must be as complete as possible.
– All project requirements must be properly defined and appropriate allowances made to meet the client's aspirations.
– The design team must have a complete understanding of its own objectives.
– All stakeholders must have contributed to the briefing process.
– An appropriate level of participation and commitment must have been allocated to the project by the client.
– Appropriate levels of authority must have been obtained from the client to review and approve the developing design.
– The client must be fully aware of the impact of their decision making.
– The cost consultant must play an active part in the developing design and the cost plan must be kept up to date.
– The project lead must ensure that the project is properly managed.
– The project controls must facilitate the progression of the developing design rather than becoming an obstacle to the process.

Chapter summary

Stage 1 Preparation and Brief should be used as an opportunity to prepare for the following stages by collecting all necessary data that the design team will require to commence the design process.

This includes collation of all available Site Information, preparation of the documentation that allows the design team to be assembled, research and debate with the client to prepare and record the Initial Project Brief, validation of the Initial Project Brief through Feasibility Studies and early definition of the project processes recorded and included within the Project Execution Plan.

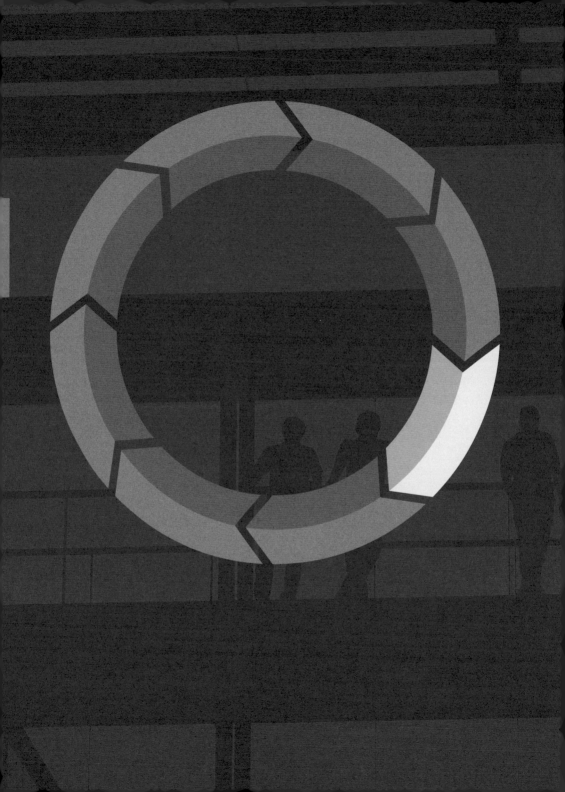

Stage 2

Concept
Design

Chapter overview

Stage 2 Concept Design is the start of the actual design activities for the design team. It is when the Initial Project Brief is developed and challenged as the emerging design strategies and ideas crystallise and become established. This chapter aims to set out the project lead's key activities and responsibilities in support of the Core Objectives of the stage.

The key coverage in this chapter is as follows:

Core Objectives

The project team

The Final Project Brief

Cost Information

Design Programme

Project Strategies

Concept Design development

Planning strategy

Client engagement and progressive sign-off

Project Execution Plan

Risk Assessments and value management

Introduction

Concept Design is the real commencement of the design process. Having established what is being asked of them through the Initial Project Brief and once the viability of the brief has been validated through Feasibility Studies, the design team is now able to consider the design response. The Concept Design stage will need to be broken down into a series of interim milestones to create a step-by-step plan that, in the first instance, identifies the objectives of each milestone, followed quickly by establishing a schedule of anticipated deliverables at each step for all design disciplines. This will ensure that appropriate input is obtained at the right time and will help everyone to understand what will be issued, by whom and when, in order to enable the objectives of the end of stage Information Exchange to be met.

An important part of project leadership is to predict inherent areas of potential conflict between design team members, such as gaps or duplication in scope, and resolve them prior to commencing design proper. This will ensure from the outset that the team can understand and agree their own mutual objectives, allowing them to pull together as a single, homogeneous unit in a truly collaborative environment.

What are the Core Objectives of this stage?

The Core Objectives of the RIBA Plan of Work 2013 at Stage 2 are:

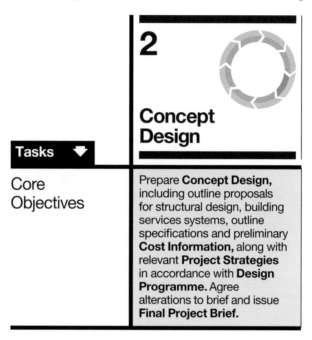

2 Concept Design	
Tasks ▼	
Core Objectives	Prepare **Concept Design,** including outline proposals for structural design, building services systems, outline specifications and preliminary **Cost Information,** along with relevant **Project Strategies** in accordance with **Design Programme.** Agree alterations to brief and issue **Final Project Brief.**

The Core Objective of this stage is to commence design activities in response to the Initial Project Brief. This stage will involve the participation of other core design team members and, depending on the scale and complexity of the project, may also involve additional consultants (eg acousticians, fire engineers and security consultants). By the end of Concept Design, the design team will have developed outline proposals to the point that they are confident that the proposals capture the essence of the Initial Project Brief. The solutions will also have been tested thoroughly by investigating the various Project Strategies that will ultimately become the functional and operational backbone of the design.

The Initial Project Brief will have been rigorously challenged to ensure that the assumptions tested during Stage 1 are still applicable and the expanded design team will overlay the next level of detailed information in collaboration with the client to form the Final Project Brief. At the end of Concept Design, the Project Programme will have been developed with input from the design team to contain a greater degree of detail covering all aspects of design, procurement, approvals and construction.

The design proposals will have been developed to a sufficient level of resolution to allow coordination between the work of the services engineer, the structural engineer and the cost consultant to confidently apply precedent cost data to the key packages of work.

Who needs to be in the project team?

There will still be a need to liaise with many stakeholders and contributors at this stage beyond the core project team and it is essential that the project lead continues to identify, notify and communicate the appropriate level of commitment required from all participants to ensure that their inputs are sought, coordinated and received in a timely manner. The design team members and third parties will have been mapped out by the project lead during the previous stage in the Project Roles Table and Contractual Tree but, as the level of input required becomes better understood, it may be necessary to include further project team members or stakeholders in the mix. The Project Roles Table will therefore need to be updated in response to the additional participants.

For smaller domestic projects it will often be sufficient to appoint only the core design team of architect (commonly also acting as the project lead, lead designer and contract administrator), structural engineer and cost consultant, with additional input from a services engineer if required.

For larger, more complex projects, the level of specialist consultant input can be substantial, as more systems and specialist accommodation require a higher level of definition. The box overleaf demonstrates the range of specialisms that can be involved in larger projects, some of whom may not be identified until later in Stage 2.

Remember, the CDM coordinator should be appointed as early as possible, and before any initial design work.

Potential members of the broader project team

- Acoustics consultant
- Facade engineer
- Design manager
- Blast engineer
- Environmental physics consultant
- Logistics consultant
- Vertical transport engineer
- Landscape architect
- Ecologist
- Fire engineer
- ICT consultant
- Access and pedestrian movement consultant
- Security consultant
- Sustainability consultant
- Traffic and transport engineer
- Exhibition fit-out designer
- Exhibition curatorial consultant
- Consultant of record (common to projects outside the UK)
- Botanist
- Ecologist
- Stone specialist
- Soil specialist
- Irrigation consultant
- Water features specialist
- Theatre consultant
- Lighting consultant
- Catering consultant
- Specification consultant

The Final Project Brief

In general terms, the Initial Project Brief will have been established during the previous stage, providing sufficient direction to the design team so that the Concept Design can be commenced.

During Concept Design, the design team will investigate the assumptions stated in the initial Project Brief in more detail and will invariably be presented with situations where the assumptions will need to be challenged as the preferred solutions evolve. This is to be expected and the Final Project Brief will have evolved from the initial Project Brief to provide more certainty in identifying the needs of the client. One of the key attributes of a professional design team is its ability to challenge and develop a brief to ensure that the optimum design solution is achieved. Evolution through Concept Design is therefore common as the design team interrogates the Initial Project Brief and suggests areas of improved functionality, operation and, of course, aesthetic.

Improving functionality

Improvements in functionality could be achieved by the introduction of dual-use spaces to reduce area, an investigation into emerging technologies to provide major benefits in the operation of the building or even a transfer from the client's operational budgets to fund more durable finishes.

Although these areas of improvement may be construed as changes to what was contained within the Initial Project Brief, their benefits warrant consideration in the evolution of the design at this stage.

The headings identified in Stage 1 (page 43) still cover the scope of the Final Project Brief but will capture further data from engagement with the client stakeholders and will essentially form the baseline from which the development of the design can be measured. This is of particular importance in ensuring that progress during the Concept Design stage is not hampered by changes in the basic premise of the Initial Project Brief. If the brief alters significantly then the design process will become too iterative as new factors are introduced, which require further research and testing rather than being part of the natural course of design development.

Fixing the Final Project Brief is essential if the design team is to make the best use of time and avoid time-consuming re-establishment of the fundamental needs of the project. Developed in this way, the Final Project Brief will become the only point of reference in determining whether a particular direction constitutes a change or a development. This is important, as the design team has based its resources, and therefore fee, on a fixed timeframe that can easily be exceeded in trying to re-establish the question rather than searching for the answer.

Changes to the Initial Project Brief during Concept Design – brief creep

Clients and architects alike may unwittingly use the Concept Design stage to help them decide on the content and scope of the project. This definition of the project must be carried out during Stage 1 as later changes to the Initial Project Brief will jeopardise the ability to meet the objectives of Concept Design within the timeframe and fee.

Cost Information

During Concept Design, it is essential that the project lead initiates a cost strategy to make sure that, during the early stages of design, costs are comprehensively managed to avoid reworking the conceptual design response late in the stage or even in following stages.

The cost consultant needs to actively participate in the design process so that cost awareness is embedded into the activities of the design team from the early formulation of conceptual ideas. Attendance for the duration of the design team meetings is recommended; partial participation, on the premise that the subject matter of the meeting does not concern the cost consultant, is not acceptable.

The establishment of a challenging but achievable budget and control of expenditure is fundamental to the successful delivery of any programme or project. As mentioned in the previous chapter, the Project Budget must be aligned with the scope and outline specifications embodied within the Initial Project Brief, and informed by market testing and sound professional advice. The Information Exchanges at the completion of Concept Design will be supported by a cost estimate which reconciles the proposed design with a contemporaneous cost plan.

Cost estimating is a formulaic assessment of the likely construction cost of a building project. A cost estimate is also an important management tool for the client, the lead designer and the design team during the early design stage, enabling the developing design to be monitored against a benchmark.

All projects begin with an idea and end by filling a need. Most projects at conceptual design require changes to produce an acceptable, workable

Cost estimate

The cost estimate accounts for all items that will generally be included in the contractor's bid. The cost estimate is prepared by breaking down the items of work using a standard format and determining the cost of each item from experience and a database of current construction cost information.

solution. The conceptual cost estimate is becoming more important to clients, design team members and contractors. It is a tool for validating the required funding and balancing the needs of a project. This tool continues to be refined during the design stages of the project.

Concept cost management is, however, an inexact process. In the absence of substantial design information, and often given genuine pressure on time available during Concept Design, there is often no way of accurately evaluating the emerging design other than by using experience and precedent data.

Communication with the cost consultant at this stage is critical and Information Exchanges must be properly planned into the process by the project lead and lead designer within the Design Programme to keep the cost consultant fully informed of the developing response and to issue the design information as it emerges. It is important not to wait for the information to be finalised or coordinated before sharing; at this stage the cost consultant will need to evaluate all manner of data to be able to form an opinion on the likely costs of the proposals. This will include obtaining information from precedent projects, early conceptual sketches and even conversations with the lead designer in order to understand their thoughts as they crystallise.

Cost management

For further information on cost management and the process recommended for use in construction projects, please visit the RICS website at www.rics.org/uk/

Design Programme

At every stage during the design process the project lead will need to make sure that the lead designer prepares a Design Programme. The Design Programme differs both graphically and in terms of content from the Project Programme as it needs to communicate a series of objectives and iterations rather than prescriptive sequential activities.

The key to successfully managing the design process during the design stages is the ability to clearly communicate not only the 'what' and the 'when' but also the 'how' within a Design Programme or a design stage plan of work. The project lead should ensure that the lead designer produces a well-defined and realistic Design Programme for the stage ahead (indicating all design team/client/third party interfaces), which will communicate a clear understanding of the objectives behind the interim milestones. This will capture not only the iterative design processes and interfaces of the entire design team but also achieve cross-consultant consensus on the anticipated interim Information Exchanges required to meet the objectives. The result is a set of mutually compatible objectives and a clear understanding of what it takes to successfully deliver a high-quality design.

The Design Programme must outline the following activities and events as a minimum:

Design Programme content

– Start and completion of each stage
– Client stage approval and sign-off period
– Client review periods
– Stage objectives
– Interim Information Exchanges by discipline
– Interim Information Exchanges objectives
– Design team meetings
– Client design review meetings
– Cost management process
– Statutory approvals process and key meetings
– Stage report production and review process

The Design Programme cannot contain all the information required to properly communicate the design process and will therefore need a suite of supporting documentation. This information will be cross-referenced in the Design Programme and will generally be made up of more detailed descriptions of the meetings strategy, content of Information Exchanges and detailed approvals deliverables, to mention just a few items.

The example of a Design Programme in figure 2.1 shows strategically how the process should be mapped out. Clear start and finish dates of the stage are established and, where possible, the end of stage client review should be shown in the context of the commencement of the following stage. The stage objectives are defined at a high level, each interim Information Exchange date is identified with associated client reviews and the objectives behind them summarised on the right-hand side of the programme. High-level activities are shown in sequence for each discipline within the design team.

The diagram in figure 2.2 was created by Eva Jiricna to explain (albeit tongue-in-cheek) the process a designer goes through before reaching a solution.

The diagram actually exemplifies very well the steps a designer takes in trying to achieve the perfect Concept Design. Unfortunately, the design process as it applies to architecture has to balance commercial, functional and operational criteria under severe pressure of time before coming close to finding the right solution. The process depicted in the diagram underlines the challenges in creating a Design Programme and the difficulties for the project lead and lead designer in managing an iterative design at Stage 2 to encompass the additional parameters of time, cost and quality.

Progress-monitoring methodology

It is important for the project lead to establish the method by which progress will be assessed at the outset of the process. The methodology will undoubtedly change as the project progresses, as certain tools for measurement are not appropriate during the early stages of design. Stage 2 is an extremely iterative process and the iterations tend to affect key Project Strategies rather than the detailed aspect of the design. This will undoubtedly have a greater impact on the perceived progress until relatively late in Stage 2, when the design tends to emerge out of the established Project Strategies. Later in the design process it may be more appropriate to measure progress by assessing the status of the Technical Design at Stage 4.

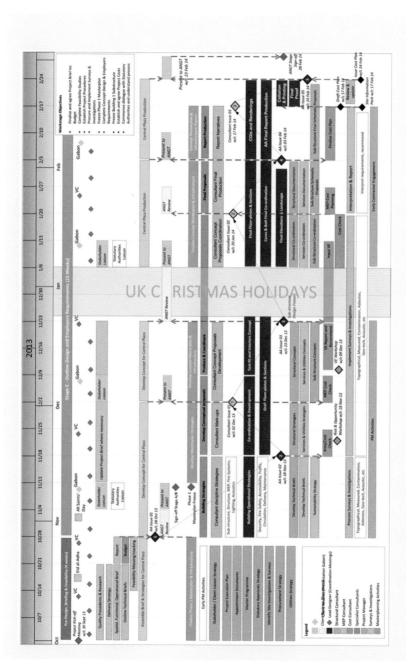

Figure 2.1 Example of a Design Programme

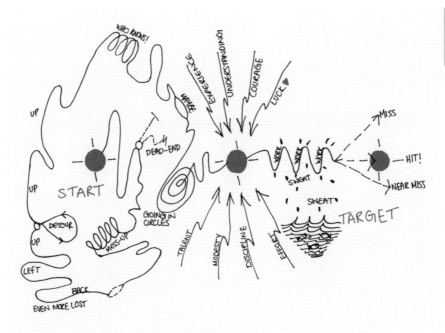

Figure 2.2   Eva Jiricna's creativity process

Eva Jiricna

For further information about Eva Jiricna please visit her website at
www.ejal.com/how.php

Project Strategies

At the commencement of Concept Design, the project lead needs to
direct the design team to ensure that its efforts are concentrated on
the appropriate priorities. The immediate priorities in the early part of
Concept Design are to build on the research and development work
completed in the previous stage. This means taking the Feasibility
Studies and working within the defined constraints to establish the
strategies from which the basis of the Concept Design is formulated.

The extent of the Project Strategies to be worked through will depend on the size and complexity of the project but will generally include the following:

Project Strategies

- **Fire engineering** – location of cores, occupancies, escape distances etc.
- **Site access** – vehicular access, pedestrian access, cycle routes etc.
- **Deliveries and waste management** – servicing strategy, waste collection, plant installation and replacement etc.
- **Accessibility and circulation** – horizontal and vertical access, cores, ramps, stairs, lifts etc.
- **Toilets and bathrooms** – related to occupancies and core locations
- **Sustainability** – solid to void ratios, orientation, renewable energy, ventilation strategies etc.
- **Phasing and expansion** – temporary conditions etc.
- **Operational strategies** – staffing, automation, maintenance etc.
- **Structural framing strategies** – pre-cast, in-situ, steel, timber etc.
- **Services strategies** – air conditioning options, mechanical and natural ventilation options, primary distribution strategy – horizontal and vertical
- **Specialist strategies** – closely related to the use of the building: shelving for libraries, seating for stadia etc.
- **Handover Strategy** – to define the process for the occupation and handover of the building to the client
- **Construction Strategy** – early consideration of how the building will be constructed
- **Health and Safety Strategy** – impact and mitigation of design and construction on health and safety

These strategies are best provided as succinct sketches, narratives and reports to be discussed in workshops with the client and the stakeholders. Sketches are appropriate because this aspect of Concept Design is about communicating and agreeing design principles rather than aesthetic considerations – the diagrams should be clear and strategic in their content and should be set out in a way that tells the client what the options are, what the project/site-specific constraints are and why various options are or are not appropriate in this instance. These Project Strategies form the backbone of the Concept Design, demonstrating how the building will work, and should be discussed and approved by the client team prior to further aesthetic development of the design.

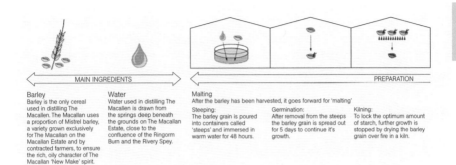

Barley
Barley is the only cereal used in distilling The Macallen. The Macallan uses a proportion of Mistrel barley, a variety grown exclusively for The Macallan on the Macallan Estate and by contracted farmers, to ensure the rich, oily character of The Macallan 'New Make' spirit.

Water
Water used in distilling The Macallen is drawn from the springs deep beneath the grounds on The Macallan Estate, close to the confluence of the Ringorm Burn and the Rivery Spey.

Malting
After the barley has been harvested, it goes forward for 'malting'

Steeping:
The barley grain is poured into containers called 'steeps' and immersed in warm water for 48 hours.

Germination:
After removal from the steeps the barley grain is spread out for 5 days to continue it's growth.

Kilning:
To lock the optimum amount of starch, further growth is stopped by drying the barley grain over fire in a kiln.

Figure 2.3   Understanding process to be accommodated

Most buildings incorporate processes, whether industrial or functional processes, that help to define both the operational requirements and the form of a particular space. Process diagrams such as the distilling process shown in figure 2.3 also form part of the building strategies and providing clear diagrams that demonstrate a clear understanding of those processes will help to integrate them into the emerging design.

The Project Strategies will be reliant on accurate Site Information so they are properly tested in context. The project lead must ensure that all Site Information is received in good time to confirm these principles.

Concept Design development

Once the Project Strategies have been discussed and agreed in the early part of Concept Design, the Initial Project Brief may have to be revisited to review its content in the context of the development of the Project Strategies. It may be that some decisions taken during this stage have affected some of the original assumptions and will need to be retested against the key components of the Initial Project Brief (budget, programme, operational aspects etc.). This is part of the process of turning the Initial Project Brief into the Final Project Brief.

Now that the Project Strategies have been established, the Concept Design studies can be progressed while, in parallel, updating the strategies that are affected by the developing design. The project lead must ensure that the lead designer concentrates on developing the Feasibility Studies prepared in Stage 1 (adjacencies, affinities, massing diagrams and stacking plans) and overlays the findings of the strategies mentioned above. This will result in a building that is designed from the inside out and addresses the client's requirements before the designer's aesthetic. Many architects and clients will be impatient at this stage and try to push forward an external architectural design solution too early in the process, resulting in an aesthetic 'solution' into which they will try to retrospectively squeeze the operational and functional aspects of the building. This course should be resisted, as it will inevitably result in the client buying in to a particular design, which lacks substantiation and will need to change later in the process. The implication of this is unnecessary and untimely disruption later in the process, putting pressure on both time and resources.

Only when the design team and the client are comfortable that they have considered all aspects of how the building works should studies commence into the appropriate architectural aesthetic. By this time, all constraints and opportunities will be known to the lead designer, whether they have arisen from the site influences and the Feasibility Studies that were investigated in the previous stage or from the operational strategies established early in the Concept Design.

This results in conceptual sketches that are grounded in reality rather than fantasy; it also makes operational compromise less likely than if the aesthetic design were to come first. At this stage of the process the developing design should be presented at an appropriate level of both detail and resolution which must be informed specifically by the principles that need to be discussed and agreed rather than a desire to present, in ultra-realistic format, what appears to be a finished product. This means returning to the first principles of architectural illustration, presenting diagrams that leave room for design development at the appropriate stage of the process. The other incentive for developing sketch illustrations rather than polished computer-generated images (CGIs) is that during Concept Design there will be a myriad of options that have to be tested before settling on an appropriate solution which can be applied to any number of different design principles. This is both time consuming and labour intensive. The design team should be making best use of the time spent with the client discussing the principles rather than preparing the material for discussion.

Concept Design objectives – stage Information Exchange requirements

- Site context and investigation studies
- Project Strategy studies (as outlined above)
- Outline site plans and site sections
- Outline floor plans and sections
- Elevational strategies, outline elevations
- 3D illustrations
- Solid working model
- Area schedules
- Outline materials specifications
- Cost estimate
- Project Programme
- Procurement strategy
- Planning strategy

It will take strong project leadership to steer both the client and the design team to develop the design in this way as for many years the process has increasingly been driven by either clients or contractors who are unfamiliar with the step-by-step objectives of an iterative but sequential design process.

Planning strategy

The project lead will need to establish the client's intent with respect to statutory authority approval for the project, as this will often determine the objectives of the stage. For example, many clients' Project Outcome or goal will simply be to obtain a planning consent that enhances the value of their site. In this case there will be pressure on the design team to aim for this objective only and avoid the resolution of issues perceived to be irrelevant to that goal. The project lead will have to explain the shortfalls of this approach in terms of obtaining a planning consent for a design that is not properly proven.

Clients will also influence where the planning application occurs in the design process. The RIBA Plan of Work 2013 recommends that the planning process occurs at the end of Stage 3 Developed Design, but speculative developers, for example, will often try to minimise the costs associated with the design team by insisting that the planning application is lodged as the key objective of Concept Design at Stage 2. While a bespoke RIBA Plan of Work can acknowledge this approach, it has inherent risks relating to potential changes as the design is developed during the following stage, potentially compromising the planning application and requiring a resubmission later in the process.

The project lead should encourage the planning strategy to be established very early in the process to ensure that all participants understand what they are striving to achieve at any given point in the programme. On larger, complex projects, especially in a urban context, it is advisable to appoint a town planning consultant as they not only specialise in planning law but also have an in-depth insight into the political aspects of gaining a planning consent.

Planning performance agreement

Larger projects will require a greater commitment in terms of time and resources from the planning authority and will therefore benefit from a planning performance agreement. This is defined as 'an agreement between a local planning authority and an applicant to provide a project management framework for handling a major planning application'. This, essentially, means procuring a dedicated service from the planning authority, which commits to a series of meetings that will provide greater certainty in the process.

To gain a better understanding of the planning process, please refer to the *RIBA Plan of Work 2013 Guide: Town Planning*, published as part of this series.

Client engagement and progressive sign-off

At all stages of projects large and small it is important to make the best use of time. It is equally important for the client to participate fully in the design process rather than sit back and wait for the stage Information Exchanges and/or final presentation by the design team. The project lead must encourage regular and structured participation by the client so that principles can be explained and agreed at the right time in the

Name of Project
Client Name

Concept Addendum Stage – Client Sign-Off Schedule

Ref.	Description	Approval sought from	Pages	Yes/No/ Comments
1	Overall massing of built form across the site			
2	Concept design (external form)			
3	Area schedule			
4	Principle of building organisation for each 'component' building – primary circulation, core locations, entrance(s) and plant location			
5	Functional adjacencies			
6	Servicing and deliveries strategy			
7	Plant rooms and distribution strategy			
8	Overall sitewide structural strategy			
9	Overall sitewide M&E strategy			
10	Procurement strategy			
11	Construction logistics strategy			
12	Approvals strategy (municipality and UPC)			

Figure 2.4   Typical client sign-off schedule

process. This means setting out the level of commitment and decision making that will be sought from the client at every design review or workshop. Obtaining progressive sign-off at regular intervals during the stage is key to an efficient design process, as it allows strategies to be agreed and 'banked' so that the following activities can progress safe in the knowledge that underlying principles will not change.

On larger projects, it is difficult to engage all stakeholders on a regular basis so it is important that the client body has a process in place to review and comment on regular Information Exchanges without impeding progress.

During each stage the project lead should initiate a decisions and approvals tracker to capture all decisions taken by the client during the Concept Design. This will prove to be a particularly useful tool, as it not only provides an audit trail of decisions taken but will also help the client to understand what they are expected to sign off following submission of what can be a comprehensive stage report. The project lead should make sure that the decisions and approvals tracker identifies only those principles of the design that need to be frozen and the reasons for doing so before entering into the following stage. This not only reduces the

Example Project
Decisions and Approvals Tracker

Issue No: 1
Date: 07/12/2011

P1 – Critical
P2 – High
P3 – Medium

Urgent/prompt action required
Action required
Agree/completed

Issue Ref	Issue	Action Owner	Action Required	Priority	RAG	Action required by (date)	Action Progress Review Date	Status	Comments/Notes

Figure 2.5 Typical decisions and approvals tracker

burden of approving design that is still being developed but also helps the client to appreciate that, in order to progress, certain principles need to be fixed at an earlier stage of the design than others, concurrently making them aware of the detrimental impact of change on time and resources at a later stage.

Project Execution Plan (PEP)

The Project Execution Plan will have been prepared during Stage 1 as explained in the previous chapter. To ensure that the Project Execution Plan reflects the practices and processes for the project as accurately and relevantly as possible, it is essential that all design team members keep the project lead updated on any changes they become aware of that need to be reflected in the document, such as updated contact details or an updated Project Programme. Equally, any inaccuracies should be reported to the project lead as soon as practicable.

The PEP is a 'live' document and needs to be regularly updated and, ideally, located online so that access to a single master document avoids the risk of superseded information circulating among the design team.

Unhelpful and cumbersome process

At all times the processes defined by the project lead should facilitate the design process as well as providing comfort to the client that everyone is pulling in the same direction to meet the Project Objectives. Too often, processes can become a burden on the design team and will place barriers in the way of progress rather than providing the framework and direction required to move the project forward.

Risk Assessments and value management

During the early period of a project, the risks and opportunities are at their most numerous and impactful as the design process is still in its infancy. Early in the process, larger adjustments in design to address risk can be made with minimal impact on progress as there are fewer established principles to potentially undo.

ID	Date Entered	Phase	Risk Description	Mitigation Options/Opportunity
001	1-Nov-06	A - Funding	Delay in finalising JV agreements causes lack of clarity over project governance	SPV agreement to be fast tracked, Draft to be circulated ASAP
004	1-Nov-06	B - Statutory Approvals	Highways approvals - protracted negotiations	Early negotiations to be undertaken. Stage C progressing early
051	24-Jan-07	A - Funding	Decision making - Delay in Client sign off and approval to proceed to next stage.	Weekly strategy meetings ongoing to minimise impact on programme
058	24-Jan-07	C - Briefing	Budget insufficient to meet Client aspirations.	Cost presentation to review ASAP
060	24-Jan-07	E - Construction	Demolition/ strip out/ decontamination programme - unable to secure early access to Bldg 62	Early contractor involvement & clear identification of decant strategy
001	24-Jan-07	A - Funding	Not maximising benefits of Capital Allowances etc	Early discussions DL/SPV following clarity on JV position
002	29-Mar-07	D - Design	Risk of conflict between University operations and Enabling works	Comprehensive plan, selection of appropriate contractor. Security of political issues appreciation
003	2-Aug-07	D - Design	Assumption – limited catering facilities in design due to assumption built into Phase 2 – risk that doesn't meet requirements and SoM cannot operate.	UofS to review and agree long/short term catering needs in conjunction with current design
004	3-Nov-06	C - Briefing	Budget insufficient & does not support sustainability/BREEAM requirements	Early audit of competition scheme to inform team & SPV
005	1-Nov-06	E - Construction	Hazardous materials in Bld 62 require extensive decommissioning - more than is planned for.	Decant/decommissioning strategy to be developed by Aug 07
006	1-Nov-06	E - Construction	Disputes - Contractor	ADR Protocols to be established
007	19-Jan-07	A - Funding	Extreme weather conditions cause delay to construction.	Dewatering proposals to be developed
008	1-Nov-06	C - Briefing	Lack of clarity over external communications	JO'K to prepare project specific communications plan
009	19-Jan-07	D - Design	Early programme constraints force early decision resulting in late design changes	JV to be established in addition to creating formal sign off procedure
010	19-Jan-07	A - Funding	Stress - key individuals fail	Key man insurance & lock in incentives to be considered
011	19-Jan-07	D - Design	Scope of changes becomes too great/too expensive	Build in design contingency to project separate from overall contingency that can be managed through stage D
012	24-Jan-07	D - Design	Design programme proves insufficient and resources can't be allocated as a result of delay in planning	Full review of resource requirements to be undertaken, mgt processes to be instigated
013	19-Jan-07	E - Construction	Failure to carry out decants to agreed timescales due to unclear strategy causing delay in works	
014	24-Jan-07	B - Statutory Approvals	Planning – discharge of reserved matters heights, areas, conflict with OPA	Expand?????
015	24-Jan-07	E - Construction	Unforeseen arise ground conditions (water fill, temporary, services, retaining wall structures)	SI to cover water table issues
016	24-Jan-07	C - Briefing	Retained structures (phase 2)	
017	25-Jan-07	B - Statutory Approvals	Delay in obtaining detailed approval from planning authority.	
018	29-Mar-07	C - Briefing	Programme durations of activities	Assess design and contractor resources. Audit undertaken
019	29-Mar-07	E - Construction	Appropriate contractor resources	Robust prequalification process
020	29-Mar-07	B - Statutory Approvals	Gateway approvals cause duplication	JV to be established ASAP
021	29-Mar-07	D - Design	Cost identification	Define scope, establish adequate contingency, assess market conditions. Provide comprehensive and robust cost plan. Obtain budget approval.
022	29-Mar-07	B - Statutory Approvals	Utilities negotiations/approvals	
023	29-Mar-07	B - Statutory Approvals	Building control sign off	Building control to be appointed for Stage D
024	29-Mar-07	B - Statutory Approvals	Fire officer approval & sign/off	
024	29-Mar-07	D - Design	Design coordination complexity: Spatial co-ordination complexity	
026	2-Aug-07	D - Design	Risk of break in continuity in short term and resources not able to move back onto project when needed – High	
027	2-Aug-07	D - Design	Risk of change in assumed procurement route will effect design programme	Early determination of procurement route required
028	2-Aug-07	D - Design	Risk of lack of engagement with end users causes late design changes	
029	2-Aug-07	D - Design	Perception of noise and vibration is higher than tolerance level	
030	2-Aug-07	D - Design	Risk of conflict between University operations (exams, animals) and construction	Move exam periods, Acoustic bunds, move venue, during demo works install acoustic panels on windows, identify sensitive areas for mitigation, sheet piling.

Figure 2.6   Typical risk register

This also means that mitigation of identified risks can be incorporated into the design with fewer consequences than if they were to be addressed later in the process. This applies equally to opportunities to enhance the design. It is therefore far better to address these issues as early as possible to avoid unnecessary delay and cost later in the process.

Risk Champion	Cost Impact	Time Impact	Probability of Event	Cost Ranking	Time Ranking	Project Ranking
SPV	Medium	High	High	6	9	9
Gifford	High	Medium	High	9	6	9
BMG	High	High	High	9	9	9
DL	Medium	High	High	6	9	9
PMU	Medium	High	High	6	9	9
DL	High	Low	High	9	1	9
B4	High	High	High	9	9	9
UoS	High	Low	High	9	3	9
B4	High	Low	Medium	6	2	6
B4	Medium	Medium	High	6	6	6
B4	High	High	Medium	6	6	6
Contractor	High	High	Medium	6	6	6
BMG	Low	Medium	High	3	6	6
B4	Medium	Medium	High	6	6	6
B4	Low	High	Medium	2	6	6
DL	High	Low	Medium	6	2	6
B4	Medium	High	Medium	4	6	6
PMU	High	High	Medium	6	6	6
LB	Medium	High	Medium	4	6	6
Gifford	High	High	Medium	6	6	6
BMG	Medium	Medium	High	6	6	6
LB	Medium	Medium	High	6	6	6
B4	High	Medium	Medium	6	4	6
B4	High	High	Medium	6	6	6
B4	Medium	Low	High	6	3	6
DL	High	High	Medium	6	6	6
Arup	High	Low	Medium	6	2	6
Grimshaw	High	High	Medium	6	6	6
PMU	High	High	Medium	6	6	6
Grimshaw	High	High	Medium	6	6	6
B4	Low	High	Medium	2	6	6
B4	Low	High	Medium	2	6	6
B4	Medium	Medium	High	6	6	6
UoS	Medium	Low	High	6	3	6
UoS	Medium	Low	High	6	3	6

The project lead should therefore initiate risk workshops and create a risk register with the whole design team to assess and mitigate any risks that can be dealt with at this early stage of the design.

If the cost management process is closely aligned with the progression of the design, then the design team will be constantly aware of the cost impacts of the developing design. The earlier the value aspects of the design relative to the emerging costs can be reviewed, the earlier major decisions can be taken to bring value and cost back into balance. If value aspects are dealt with later, then the emphasis in addressing cost overruns will be on cost cutting, which results in value being compromised.

It is incumbent on the project lead to ensure that these activities are blended into the early design process in order to optimise their impact, while not being detrimental to the Final Project Brief.

Chapter summary   2

Stage 2 Concept Design should be seen as an amalgamation of the core Project Strategies that validate the outcomes of both the Feasibility Studies and the site investigations from the previous stage. The building must therefore be designed from the inside out to avoid shoehorning the functionality of the building into a desirable but inappropriate aesthetic design solution.

Also during Concept Design the Initial Project Brief will need to be developed into the Final Project Brief. It is essential that this is the consequence of adding more detail and reconciling strategies rather than fundamentally changing the principles of the brief. If the latter is allowed to happen unchecked then the design process will be less efficient as work completed in Stage 1 will need to be revisited.

The effort placed on presentation should be put into the context of what the information to be presented is trying to achieve. CGIs often have the effect of presenting the design as a fait accompli, appearing to be more resolved than it actually is or should be at this stage of the process. Project Strategies should therefore have the ability to be adjusted quickly and painlessly to respond to the iterative process of conceptual design.

Communicating the objectives of Concept Design falls to the project lead and the structured engagement of the client and their progressive buy-in to the design should be carefully targeted to make sure that they fully understand the objectives of this stage.

Developed Design

Chapter overview

Stage 3 Developed Design is the development stage of the conceptual design, including coordinated and updated proposals for structural design, building services systems, outline specifications, Cost Information and Project Strategies in accordance with the Design Programme.

The key coverage in this chapter is as follows:

Integration of Project Strategies

Developed Design studies

BIM integration

Interim reporting

End of stage reporting

Undertake third party consultations as required

Project Programme and progress monitoring

Change Control Procedures

Value management

Construction and Health and Safety Strategies

Introduction

There are more activities contained within the new Stage 3 relative to the old Work Stage D as defined in previous versions of the Plan of Work. The key adjustment is that Developed Design now advances a portion of what was the old Detailed Design (Work Stage E), achieving a greater level of detailed development and resolution than the old Work Stage D. The Project Programme will need to accommodate the increased effort and activities in this stage. Fee and resource allowances will also have to reflect this amendment in the initial fee proposals as the projected effort required to meet the objectives of this stage has increased. Stage 3 can be a major milestone, depending on the procurement route, often forming the basis of Employer's Requirements, and it is most commonly the stage at which a planning application will need to be submitted.

What are the Core Objectives of this stage?

The Core Objectives of the RIBA Plan of Work 2013 at Stage 3 are:

Tasks ▼	
Core Objectives	Prepare **Developed Design**, including coordinated and updated proposals for structural design, building services systems, outline specifications, **Cost Information** and **Project Strategies** in accordance with **Design Programme**.

Developed Design must build on the principles established during Concept Design rather than 'developing' the design in isolation from the work completed in the previous stage. During Concept Design the Project Strategies will have been considered in the context of the specific site constraints. The principles of these strategies will now be embedded within the design and must be taken to the next level of detailed resolution to ensure that they are fully integrated and coordinated as part of the developing design.

The roles and responsibilities of the project lead are essential to the organisation of the design team and the planning and monitoring of the objectives and activities in support of the design. On large projects, the relationship between the project lead and the lead designer is crucial, as one informs the activities of the other. There must be a clear understanding between the two to make sure that both are heading in the same direction.

During this stage, the activities of the other core members of the design team will intensify as the architectural design becomes more settled. As the design team moves away from conceptual sketches and the design becomes more crystallised, the use of BIM technologies is also now beginning to be more integrated into the design process.

The structural engineering input up to this point will have related to testing strategies to establish the broader principles of framing options, grids and spatial allowances in terms of achievable floor-to-floor heights and external walls. The services engineering input will, equally, have concentrated on dealing with the selection of appropriate environmental systems, their impact on spatial allowances and the provision and distribution of plant room areas, all of which will be closely linked with the sustainability strategy proposed in Stage 2.

During Developed Design it is also essential for the cost consultant to adopt a pre-emptive approach to cost management by actively participating in the design process, becoming familiar with the developing design and preventing the design team from straying from the cost parameters established during Concept Design. The method of establishing cost will also change during Developed Design as sufficient information will be produced to allow the cost consultant to fully understand the design and cost the scheme on an elemental basis.

Other than developing the design to the next level of resolution, the ultimate objective of Developed Design depends on both the procurement strategy and the planning strategy, both of which were touched upon in the preceding chapter and will be explained in more detail later in this chapter.

The key role of the project lead at this stage will be to establish the objectives of the stage as they relate to the variables of procurement and town planning, allowing the lead designer to focus on the design and coordination activities in support of the defined objectives. The size and complexity of the project will determine whether the roles of the project lead and the lead designer require independent focus. On smaller, less complex projects the roles are combined and commonly carried out by the architect.

Design development vs change

It is important to be aware of the difference between design development and change. The definition of change relies on an in-depth understanding of the Final Project Brief by all participants and can be a contentious issue that needs to be dealt with firmly and diplomatically by the project lead. Often, design changes are instigated by the design team, as further investigative work during Developed Design prompts ideas that could not be considered in such detail during Concept Design.

The approach to change varies in virtually every project with some clients and design teams happy to accommodate change if it is deemed to improve the emerging design. This should not prevent the issue being properly elevated to the client for discussion in order to ensure that all implications in respect of cost, programme and brief are properly considered. Both the client and the design team must be happy that the issue has been resolved, allowing all parties to move forward knowing that this will not resurface as an issue further down the line, when unpicking the 'change' could present disproportionate disruption to the design process.

While this approach may constitute design development (because a given element was not properly defined in the brief) it has an impact on various key Project Objectives and therefore needs to be flagged at the earliest opportunity as a potential change to avoid unnecessary disruption later in the process.

Volume

A common example of the interpretation of design development versus change arises from the introduction of grander spaces within the design. Volume is often not properly defined in a project brief and therefore frequently insufficient allowance will be made within the Project Budget. If the design team, in developing the design, decides that a sense of place could be improved by incorporating significant volume, then this could have an impact on cost, operations and, potentially the Construction Programme.

Integration of Project Strategies

At Stage 3, all of the Project Strategies that were identified in either narrative or sketch form during Stage 2 will need to be coordinated into the developing design as part of the proposed general arrangement layouts. These strategies will have informed the layouts during the earlier design process so it is important that they have been agreed during Stage 2 to be appropriate to the project requirements. This will undoubtedly require several iterations as, often, when they are collectively integrated into the layouts there will be conflicting requirements that will need to be assessed and resolved according to priority and suitability.

Developed Design studies

As the name suggests, it is during Stage 3 that the Concept Design is developed to a greater level of detail and resolution in terms of the coordinated input of the core design team. If not already defined during Stage 1, the project lead instigates at the commencement of Stage 3 an enhanced level of detailed inputs in relation to structure, services and any relevant specialist contributions and initiates a collaborative strategy at the commencement of the stage for all to follow.

The use of BIM during Stage 3 is becoming more common and the government is encouraging its wider use by setting targets to have all centrally procured projects achieve Level 2 BIM by 2016, although it is unlikely that this aspirational target will be met. BIM in the context of the design process will be explained in slightly more detail in the following chapter but it is also covered in more depth in the *RIBA Plan of Work 2013 Guide: Design Management*. To dispel an industry myth, it does not significantly alter the design process but does necessitate a greater level of information exchange, communication, collaboration and earlier fixity than has historically been experienced in the 2D world of computer-aided design (CAD).

The developing design will generally move up a scale in Stage 3, so that a greater understanding of the detail configurations and their design interfaces can be achieved. Although the CAD model is effectively constructed at a scale of 1:1, the level of detail contained in the output of the drawings is enhanced at this stage of development to avoid later conflicts. This entails interrogating the systems proposed for the

Variable objectives – Employer's Requirements

It is important during Stage 3 to establish some of the variable objectives that will inform the key activities and purpose of the stage. The anticipated procurement route will affect the final Information Exchange as it is not unusual for design and build contractors to be appointed on the basis of the available Stage 3 design information (in fact, there are examples of contractors being appointed at Stage 2 or even Stage 1) – this pack of information is usually referred to as the Employer's Requirements (ERs). The main difference between the content of a Stage 3 report and a set of Employer's Requirements is the level of detail and resolution embedded within the design. Aside from the core design documentation (plans, elevations, sections) the ERs will need to cover in sufficient detail all areas of the design that are particularly precious to the client and design team that otherwise could be left until later in a traditional procurement route. This is because the contractor will base their scope of work and price on the information available at Stage 3, so it is in the client's interest to have defined to a greater level of detail elements of fit-out, finishes and fixtures, fittings and equipment.

envelope, roofs, internal walls, ceilings and floors in order to establish a better position from which to coordinate the works.

At this stage, the iterations need to be more focused, both in terms of minimising substantial divergence from the design concept and in terms of the time and resources required to work towards detailed resolution. This means ensuring that the design team does not unnecessarily undo work carried out in Stage 2 but concentrates on taking the design to a higher level of understanding. The general arrangements should therefore only change to reflect an increased understanding of the detail that informs them.

The design studies at this stage should therefore pursue an enhanced understanding of the spatial and technical requirements at a larger scale. They can then be integrated back into the general arrangements to identify areas of potential conflict that can, in turn, be investigated and resolved. This process involves the design team working together through workshops and coordination meetings to gradually move towards the resolution of the design.

Design studies: ceilings

Ceiling profiles within the scheme should be examined at a greater scale to incorporate specific architectural details and MEP/structural engineering inputs, which will need to be reflected in the general arrangement drawings to ensure that coordination of the design is maintained.

It is useful at an early stage in Stage 3 to storyboard the final Information Exchange, which is generally in the form of a formal report. By mapping out for each discipline every page of the report in sketch form, it is easier to plan the activities that support the required input to the report.

Stage sign-off vs design freeze

It is not always necessary to obtain blanket approvals to design stages, especially when the burden and perceived commitment by the client to these approvals sometimes results in delay and protracted process in achieving them. Far more important to both the design team and the client is to understand the purpose of the approval and what it means in terms of design freeze to allow the next stage to progress on a clear understanding of which principles will have a significant impact on the Project Programme if undone at a later stage in the design process. Design freezes need to be properly explained to the client as part of the progressive design process – it stands to reason that structural grids, for example, should be defined as early as possible as the impact of changing them later in the process is disproportionately large.

The iterative design process – striving for design perfection

As uncomfortable as it may be to hear, building design is a balance between the creativity expected of architects and the commercial awareness expected by clients. A real risk in Stage 3 Developed Design is the genuine desire to continuously improve the design. This is generally not a problem if the design development retains the principles set out in Stage 2; however, the temptation to revisit these principles can cause serious conflict between the architect, the client and the remainder of the design team. Engineers, cost consultants and specialists alike

Stage sign-off vs design freeze (*continued*)

will be reluctant to continually update their documentation and, in most cases, use the architect's indecision to justify waiting until the design settles down before providing drawn input. This should not be allowed to happen and the project lead must encourage the architect to minimise the iterations as the design process unfolds.

BIM integration

As mentioned above, BIM is covered in *RIBA Plan of Works 2013 Guide: Design Management*, but it is worth introducing the subject to project leads to help them decide, in conjunction with the client, whether BIM is a requirement for the project. The decision to proceed with BIM central to the design will have been taken in Stage 1, but it is described in this chapter as more often than not design teams are still determining the most comfortable point at which to integrate BIM into the process. Advanced BIM teams will have started the process using the principles of BIM at the outset of Stage 2. However, many design teams are used to developing the Concept Design in a more fluid environment and therefore leave full BIM integration to Stage 3.

BIM is an in-depth database that not only contains the building elements in 3D format but also geometric, visual, dimensional, process and specification information. If the software is the means of accessing and manipulating a building information model, then the data-rich content is the heart of information management.

Properly managed, BIM will reduce the residual data loss often experienced when the design information is passed from design team, to construction team and to building owner/operator, by allowing each group to add to, and reference back to, all the information they need during their period of ownership of the BIM model. To put it simply, without the embedded information, a BIM model is little more than a 3D model, as interpreted by many people.

This information about the objects allows designers (architects and engineers) to build an 'intelligent' digital model of their design within a

CAD environment that enables them to explore a project's key physical and functional characteristics digitally – before it is built.

The maturity model suggests that some subcontractors and suppliers will want improved levels of development of BIM integration – the inclusion of Level 3 recognises this ambition without specifying the expectations in respect of timeframe. The definition of Level 3 is also subject to much discussion and will undoubtedly be subject to further development.

BIM level definitions

Level 0
Unmanaged CAD, in 2D, with paper (or electronic paper) data exchange.

Level 1
Managed CAD in 2D or 3D format with a collaborative tool providing a common data environment with a standardised approach to data structure and format.

Level 2
A federated BIM model in a common data environment, held in separate discipline 'BIM' tools with data attached. This level of BIM may utilise 4D construction sequencing and/or 5D cost information.

Level 3
A fully integrated and collaborative process enabled by 'web services' and compliant with emerging Industry Foundation Class (IFC) standards. This level of BIM will utilise 4D construction sequencing, 5D cost information and 6D project life cycle management information.

BIM allows construction companies to reduce risk and cost in the construction process through a better understanding of the design and construction sequence while also promoting more effective collaboration with their supply chain. It also allows facilities and asset managers (the owners or occupiers) to more rapidly and effectively take on and manage space, maintenance and running costs for their portfolio.

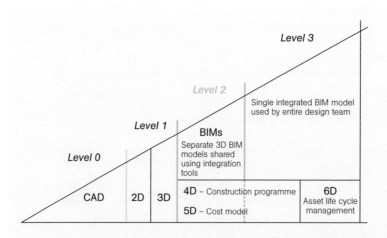

Figure 3.1   BIM maturity diagram and timescales (based on Bew and Richards, 2012)

Despite the worthy aspirations of the government, there are some industry leaders who have concerns that the industry may not be ready to meet the target by 2016.

BIM vs 3D modelling

BIM is a much misinterpreted idea. To many clients, consultants and architects BIM is simply the use of 3D CAD modelling by all members of the design team. However, BIM is far more than this and it is important that the project lead ensures that there is a common interpretation of the level of BIM implementation to be utilised on the project. BIM has several levels of implementation, which can incorporate attributed data, such as component specification, programme, cost and facilities management data. The design team must be aware of the aspirations relating to BIM levels at the outset to ensure the BIM model is configured in a way that can accommodate all anticipated information to be embedded in the model and that the expertise to extract this information is available.

Interim reporting

This and the following section define the structure and content of interim reports (monthly reports) and reports to be produced to confirm the extent and nature of work completed at a particular stage.

A monthly reporting process (or any given frequency determined by the project lead in collaboration with the client) must be established early to ensure that all design team members understand the objectives of the reports to be prepared. These reports can be instigated in Stage 2; however, the conceptual design process is less linear during the early stages and therefore progress is more difficult to define. The reports should be succinct but comprehensive and should provide no more information than is necessary for the project lead and client to understand the key issues arising at any given time. These reports will generally be collated and coordinated from all consultants by the lead designer. On larger, more complex projects, the project lead will receive, review and add an executive summary, extracting the salient issues from the report to bring exceptional issues to the client's attention without overwhelming them with the more mundane mechanics of the design development.

Monthly report contents

Typical subject matter for inclusion in monthly reports can be (authors of sections given in italics):

- Executive summary – *project lead*
  o Successes
  o Concerns
  o Decisions
  o Information outstanding
- Design and quality matters – *lead designer*
- Progress status – *lead designer*
- Risk and opportunity – *project lead*
- Finance – *project lead*
  o Key budgets
  o Cashflow
  o Contract awards and additional services
- Client issues – *lead designer*

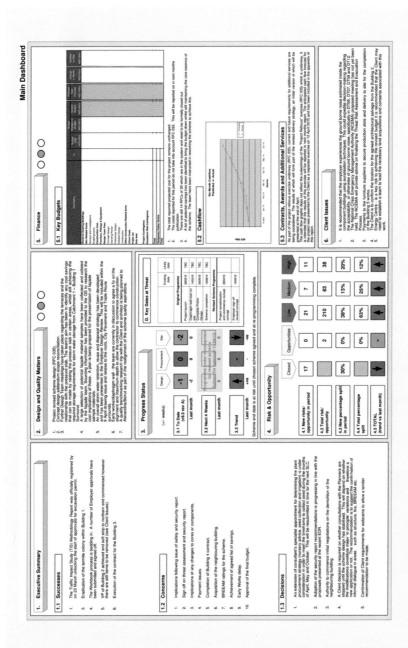

Figure 3.2 Example monthly dashboard

If the reports provide too much information then they will fail in their ability to alert the project lead (and subsequently the client) to issues that require attention as this information can be buried in burdensome narratives. The reporting process should emphasise the benefits of looking forward rather than concentrating on historical events. This will save time in the preparation of the reports but will also act as a pre-emptive tool to allow problems to be avoided rather than time being spent recording historical activities. A useful template for this is the 'dashboard' which, as the name suggests, highlights key issues for consideration with reference to further material should a deeper understanding be required. The content of the dashboard will vary depending on the size and complexity of the project and certain key performance indicators required by the client; however, the topics suggested above should be covered regardless of the project scale.

End of stage reporting

For end of stage reports, the project lead must determine the structure and scope of the report that best suits the needs of the client and ensure that it is produced at the correct time and is structured suitably to obtain appropriate sign-off of its content. The design team will have to produce a stage report at the end of Stage 3 (and later stages if agreed with the client). These will normally be in the form of a formal written illustrated report, defining the scope of the design work undertaken at that stage, as agreed with the client.

A less formal approach to documentation may be arranged, if appropriate, and must be agreed by the project lead and the client. The report should comprehensively cover the project to a level of detail appropriate to the stage, clearly establishing the degree to which the design is fixed, and what is necessary to complete the design.

The main purpose of the report is to obtain the agreement of the client (as well as others in the design team and other stakeholders) regarding the status of the design at the stage when the report is issued, thus providing a firm basis for proceeding with the next stage. Therefore, formal sign-off should be obtained. This can be in the form of a sign-off sheet bound into the report or, for example, an exchange of emails with a client representative authorised to approve the design. The next stage should not proceed without this formal sign-off, unless specifically agreed by the project lead or by the conclusion of a client meeting.

The following schedule indicates the typical content and structure for reports at Developed Design stage. Supporting documentation such as drawings, sketches, models and specifications should be referred to using clear references (eg, drawing references including revision).

End of stage reporting

Developed Design report (Stage 3)

1. **Cover sheet contents**
2. **Summary**
3. **Sign-off**
4. **Design**
   a. Statement describing developments since previous stage
   b. Site plan
   c. Building envelope sections, elevations
   d. Building concept sketches
   e. Floor plans, including main blocking principles
   f. Core plans, special area plans
   g. Interior design principles for main functional areas
   h. Interior design concept sketches
   i. Materials concept boards (images)
   j. Outline materials specification
5. **Services**
   a. Services statement update/specification notes
   b. Services outline drawings showing principles
6. **Structures**
   a. Structures statement update/specification notes
   b. Structural drawings demonstrating principles
7. **Specialist consultants**
   a. Summary of any fundamental issues that must be signed off at this stage
   b. Strategy for: catering, security, acoustics, other specialist areas
8. **Process**
   a. Programme for remaining stages. Key activities and sign-offs: future stages
   b. Briefing process description: Stage 3 phasing diagrams/statement if applicable
9. **Technical**
   a. Schedule of areas
   b. Project risk identification
   c. Environmental statement, schedule of areas
   d. Cost plan summary, schedule of areas
   e. Project Risk Assessments (CDM)
   f. Risk Assessments (other risks)

End of stage reporting (*continued*)

     g. Environmental statement update
     h. Statutory approvals: current position
  10. Drawings
     a. Schedule of drawings; include complete drawing reference and
       revision for all drawings which form part of the report

Alternatively, reduced copies of the drawings can be bound into the report (the future integration of BIM may reduce this requirement as the BIM model itself becomes the primary information exchange).

Undertake third party consultations as required

During Stage 2 Concept Design there will have been a significant level of third party consultation that will have informed the developing design. This will include consultations with major stakeholders, such as the various departments of a client body, statutory authorities, local interest groups and, on the larger, high-profile projects, even public consultations.

During Stage 3 there will still be a requirement to consult; however, as the design is becoming more fixed, these consultations will take the form of validating the design rather than informing it. It is useful to track the third party consultations from the outset to make sure that all inputs have been properly considered and responded to. This will usually take the form of an Excel spreadsheet to provide a single point of reference for all comments and provide a live status of their incorporation into the design.

The statutory approvals process inevitably presents considerable risk to the progress of a project unless proper consultation, consideration and planning is carried out at an early stage of the project. The point at which the client decides to submit the project for planning consent varies. It can be submitted at the end of Stage 2 or, more commonly, at the end of Stage 3. Submitting at Stage 2 carries with it inherent risk that the design has not reached a sufficient level of fixity and may require later amendments to the obtained consent. The planning application process is covered in detail in *RIBA Plan of Work 2013 Guide: Town Planning* in this series so this chapter will simply give an overview of the building control objectives.

Building regulations are designed to safeguard the wellbeing of people in and around buildings as well as to ensure that buildings are safe, healthy, accessible and sustainable for current and future generations.

Building control should not be confused with planning. Building Regulations approval does not mean the same as obtaining planning permission for the work. In the same way, being granted planning permission is not the same as taking action to ensure that the work complies with Building Regulations. Building control legislation covers the structure, construction and the health and safety aspects of buildings. Planning legislation covers the use, size and appearance of buildings and how they affect the street scene and other aspects of urban planning.

The building regulations cover matters such as structural stability, fire safety, conservation of fuel and power and access and facilities for disabled persons. Compliance will involve checking plans of the proposed works and then carrying out inspections of the work on site as it proceeds.

The project or 'building work' will be subject to, and must comply with, the Building Regulations. To help achieve compliance with the regulations, the project lead, in conjunction with the client, must decide whether to use one of two types of building control service:

I the local authority building control service, or
I an approved inspector's building control service.

If the approved inspector route is chosen, then they will take on responsibility for plan checking and inspection of the design and building work. The project lead and the approved inspector must jointly notify the relevant local authority on what is referred to as an initial notice. Once this notice has been accepted by the local authority (usually after a period of five days) the responsibility for plan checking and site inspections will formally rest with the approved inspector.

Both the local authority and an approved inspector are able to carry out the following building control activities:

I advise the project lead on how the Building Regulations apply to a specific project
I check the drawings
I issue a plans certificate (if requested)

l   inspect the work as it progresses, and
l   issue a final certificate.

It is equally important to map out the detailed process within the Project Programme, identify the challenges and pinch points, understand their impacts on progress and, if it is not possible to mitigate them, coordinate these constraints with the various stages of the Project Programme.

Other third parties whose opinions could present risks to the project if not consulted early in the process could be listed as follows:

l   funders/investors (Heritage Lottery Fund, Higher Education Funding Council for England etc.)
l   potential tenants
l   building user-groups
l   local action/resident groups
l   Cabe (Commission for Architecture and the Built Environment) (Design Council)
l   English Heritage.

Project Programme and progress monitoring

The principles of the Project Programme have been outlined at Stage 1 Preparation and Brief (pages 54–7); however, the method that the project lead employs to monitor progress against the Project Programme deserves some attention, as interpretations of how effective the use of time has been can vary widely depending on the perspective of those doing the monitoring.

The objective of progress monitoring is to establish 'where are we now' and therefore, as outlined in Stage 1, it is essential to have a robust, realistic and achievable programme against which progress measurements can be made.

The following points describe the key principles of progress monitoring:

l   Progress should be measured on a regular basis.
l   The same programme must be used at each point of progress measurement.
l   The project lead must record progress of all activities contained in the Project Programme.

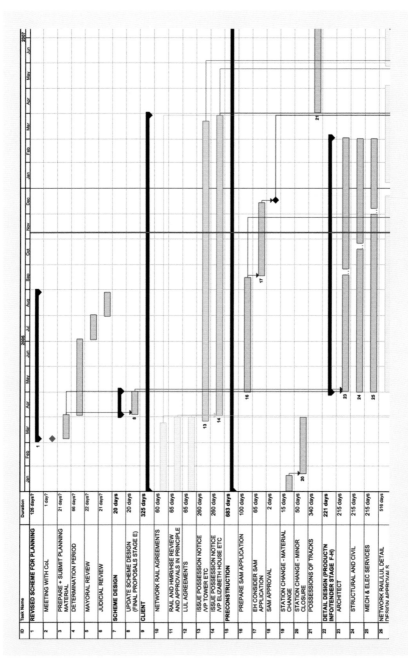

Figure 3.3 Example Project Programme

- Monitoring must be objective, eg production rate achieved vs rate planned/required, rather than how much has been spent.
- Monitoring must be transparent – the figures used and comments made against any activities should be clear and made available to all appropriate project stakeholders.
- Accurate records must be maintained, which can be referred to during future reporting and in the event of any disputes that may arise.
- The progress date and the programme on which it is based must be clearly stated.
- Reports must be in a format and level of detail appropriate to the recipient, the stage of the project and the certainty of the Project Programme itself.
- Reports must be presented to and discussed with key stakeholders – not just 'issued'.
- Reports must be in a consistent format for each reporting period.

It should be noted that during the early stages of the design process, design is not a linear process and therefore progress cannot be monitored on the basis of information prepared relative to the percentage of time completed. That is to say that, while emerging design ideas still form a large objective of the stage, it is difficult to plan exactly when these will crystallise and therefore it is unreasonable for the Project Programme to seek to dictate a definitive point in time for these to occur. This does not provide carte blanche for the lead designer to ignore progress but will allow some flexibility for re-sequencing events and reallocating resources to take account of when these enhancements occur.

Linear measurement

The design team is unlikely to have completed 30% of the design documentation at a point 30% of the way through the Design Programme – it is not unusual for as much as 60% of the actual documentation production to be completed during the final 30% of the Design Programme to allow sufficient time to think, design, sketch and coordinate the developing ideas during the earlier phases.

Change Control Procedures

Change will inevitably arise during the course of a project and, provided that an effective and robust management regime is in place, it is not something that should be feared.

The implications of change will also depend on the stage of the project; however, it is normal for a Change Control Procedure to be initiated during Stage 3, Developed Design. Change brought about by discussion and definition of detailed project requirements early in the process is to be encouraged if the best solution to the client's needs is to be identified. However, change during the later stages can be disruptive and costly.

Educating users and clients early in the process that untimely change will have significant implications is a key task of the project lead. Efforts need to be directed to demonstrating that time spent accurately defining their needs early in the process will be of greater benefit as the implications are likely to be more manageable, and therefore lead to greater certainty during implementation.

Whatever the stage of the project, the approach is the same:

I What is the change?
I What will it affect?
I Will it create a delay (to the design or construction period)?

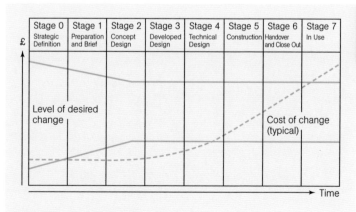

Figure 3.4   Impact of late change

| Will it add to the project cost?
| Does it offer a better solution than currently exists?
| Notwithstanding the implications of the change, does it represent greater value?

As the decision to implement a change is, in most cases, dependent on the cost and/or time implications, it is important to ensure that the project always has a clear cost plan and Project Programme against which to measure the implications.

Pro forma change management forms are completed by the originators of the change and circulated to various parties to collect the data for assessment before a final decision on whether or not to incorporate the change is taken.

Only changes that can demonstrate value or fix mistakes/discrepancies should be taken forward. Any member of the design team can raise a change but the project lead carries the responsibility for recording these. A change may be anything that impacts on the defined project scope – whether time, cost or other effect – with formal Change Control Procedures commencing at the start of Stage 3 using the signed-off Stage 2 documentation as a baseline.

Any change to the baseline documentation, drawings, specifications and/ or the assumptions on which the cost plan and/or Project Programme are based, should be recorded and the impact assessed (in terms of cost and programme) so that the change can be reviewed by the team, approved or rejected by the client and then, if approved, incorporated into the next financial report and/or programme issue.

The principal control document is the change control form (although this can have many names). The purpose of this form is to:

| alert all parties to the existence and nature of any potential change
| provide a structured means of reporting the potential implications of that change on cost, programme and any other relevant criteria
| provide a basis for the decision to approve or reject the proposed change and inform the adjustment of the budget, programme and other criteria as necessary, and
| trigger the issue of the relevant instruction to cover any approved changes.

Project Title

Client Name

Request For Change Register

Issue No:

Date:

Reason for Change Categories:

1 Briefing change
2 Change to signed off Design Stage
3 Design development
4 Safety/operational requirement
5 Regulatory requirement
6 Quality improvement
7 Cost saving
8 Site problem
9 Error/omission
10 Other

Status Options

Rejected
Open
Instructed

Request For Change No.	Date opened	Description of change	Reason for change (1-10)	Project Stage	Initiator	Owner	Summary of Impact		Status of RFC	Incorporation of Change		
							Cost	Time		Instruction required by	Instruction reference	Incorporated

Example change control register

1 of 1

Figure 3.5   Example change control register

A change control request should be raised by any party whenever they consider that there is, or may be, a variation to the brief or any principle deemed to be approved during the Stage 2 design approval process.

The change control register is the subsidiary control document and will be maintained by the project lead. Its purpose is to provide a summary of the status of all change control forms at any time, and to enable the design team to focus its attention on those requiring action. It is equally important on a small project to have a clear understanding of the status of change, as the knock-on effect of change can be just as disruptive to the progress of design in domestic projects. The decision whether to incorporate changes or not, based on a clear understanding of all the implications, should in every case lie with the client.

Value management

Where there is a budget deficit and a full team review is required, it is the responsibility of the project lead to manage and control a process of value management. The team needs to work closely with the cost consultant as well as the remainder of the project team, which should include the contractor (if appointed) and client body to achieve a total 'buy-in' to the process. The relationship between the project lead, lead designer and the cost consultant is crucial in order to drive the process to a successful conclusion. By extending the requirement for consolidated input to the entire design team the project lead is able to ensure that the relevant expertise is sought and that the client's expectations are met.

The project lead should at all times actively challenge the cost consultant to ensure that the cost plan figures are accurate for the current market and location and should encourage and even facilitate the engagement of subcontractors to test the cost plan allowances.

The review of the design and cost plan should highlight areas that the project lead feels may benefit from further investigation. It is important for this 'value engineering' to be assessed in the appropriate context relevant to the specific project objectives. Depending on these objectives, the project lead will need to bear in mind any cost-driven requirements and any impact on fees, in balance with any savings identified.

The project documentation should be interrogated to ensure that there has not been any 'design creep' and that the solutions being offered are the most practical and cost effective. It is always important at this stage to refer to the approved Final Project Brief to ensure that nothing has been detracted from it in the quest for financial savings. However, there may some options which would require deviation from the Final Project Brief and, if these are to be considered/proposed, they should be highlighted for approval.

The value management process during Stage 3 has the benefit of being early enough in the process that incorporation of value added ideas will have a minimal disruptive effect on the programme. This assessment will identify a clear list of proposed items, which can be presented to the client body.

Value engineering vs cost cutting

It is important to understand the difference between value engineering and cost cutting. The former is a process which attempts to maintain the essence of the Final Project Brief but seeks to add value in areas that may not have been properly considered by the design team. The consequence is not in every case a cost saving, but must result in demonstrable added value. Cost cutting generally requires some compromise to the Final Project Brief.

Construction and Health and Safety Strategies

The design team is in a unique position to reduce the risks that arise during construction work and has a key role to play in the implementation of safe design. At each stage, designers from all disciplines can make a significant contribution by identifying and eliminating hazards, and reducing likely risks from hazards where elimination is not possible.

The earliest decisions of the design team fundamentally affect the health and safety of construction work. It is therefore vital for the project lead to address health and safety from an early stage in the development of the design.

The design team's responsibilities extend beyond the construction phase of a project. The health and safety of those who will maintain, repair, clean, refurbish and eventually remove or demolish all or part of a structure as well as the health and safety of users of workplaces will need to be considered.

The design team should:

I make sure that it is competent and adequately resourced to address the health and safety issues likely to be involved in the design – this issue needs to be addressed at the appointment stage
I check that the client is aware of their duties
I during the design process, avoid foreseeable risks to those involved in the construction and future use of the structure and, in doing so, it should eliminate hazards (so far as is reasonably practicable) and reduce risk associated with those hazards which remain
I provide adequate information about any significant risks associated with the design
I coordinate its work with that of others in order to improve the way in which risks are managed and controlled.

The project lead should instigate regular reviews of the design with all members of the design team to ensure that proper consideration is given to buildability, usability and maintainability. When considering buildability, meetings should include the contractor (if appointed) so that difficulties associated with construction can be discussed and solutions agreed before the work begins. When discussing usability and maintainability, involving the client or those who will be responsible for operating the building or structure will mean that proper consideration can be given to the health and safety of those who will maintain and use the structure once it has been completed. Doing this during the design stage will result in significant cost savings for the client, as rectifying mistakes after the structure has been built is almost always an expensive business.

In addition to the duties outlined above, when the project is notifiable under the CDM regulations, the project lead should:

I ensure that the client has appointed a CDM coordinator prior to commencing design work
I ensure that design work is not started, other than initial design work, unless a CDM coordinator has been appointed

I cooperate with the CDM coordinator, principal contractor and any other designers or contractors as necessary for each of them to comply with their duties. This includes providing any information needed for the pre-construction information or health and safety file.

Chapter summary 3

Stage 3 Developed Design is the next logical step in a process that starts at the generic and moves towards the specific as design strategies become fixed. It should be a natural development and integration of the strategies established and approved at the completion of Stage 2 Concept Design and should therefore not be treated as an opportunity to revisit these principles and potentially undo the good work done in Stage 2.

As a consequence, the design studies should be more specific, involve multidisciplinary inputs and focus on integrating these into the developing design solution. Stage 3 is less about options and more about developing the preferred option established at the completion of Stage 2.

The approvals process will be implemented for both building control and planning consent at this stage and detailed discussions with statutory authorities will become more focused as the design is tested for regulatory compliance.

The client's objectives should have been established prior to commencement of the stage to allow the project lead to concentrate the efforts of the design team on the appropriate outcomes to meet these expectations – planning applications and early design and build contractor appointment can be key objectives of this stage.

If contractor procurement is a requirement at the completion of this stage, then a comprehensive set of Employer's Requirements will be required, which will alter the extent of information exchanged at the end of the stage.

The integration of cost management during Stage 3 is particularly important and the process of engagement with the cost consultant should be discussed with them to ensure their participation to obtain a full understanding of the design. The cost consultant should now have sufficient information to cost the proposals on an elemental basis rather than establishing the costs on a per metre rate.

Technical Design

Chapter overview

At Stage 4 the Technical Design is prepared in accordance with the Design Responsibility Matrix and Project Strategies to include all architectural, structural and building services information, specialist subcontractor design and specifications, in accordance with the Design Programme. The information produced at this stage must be sufficient for the contractor to both price accurately and, subsequently, build the works. If any contractor's designed portions are identified in the Building Contract then the design team will be producing design intent drawings from which the contractor will complete the technical design.

The key coverage in this chapter is as follows:

Core Objectives

Technical Design activities

Design Programme

Detailed specifications

Discharge of planning conditions

Contract documents

Package definition

Impact of procurement on technical design activities

Samples procurement – mock-up definition

Pre-tender estimate

Tender documentation – key content

Tender reviews

Contractor design submittals

Construction Strategy

Introduction

Generally, at Stage 4 the Developed Design from Stage 3 is translated into precise technical documentation, sufficient to allow for pricing and for construction of the proposed works. Depending on the chosen procurement route the documentation will be produced either by the design team, the contractor or their subcontractors to increase cost certainty by testing the design information with their supply chain. Further explanation of this can be found in the *RIBA Plan of Works 2013 Guide: Design Management*.

It is, however essential that the time in this stage is used to develop the details that supported the Developed Design and coordinate them with the engineering disciplines and those of the specialist subcontractors with design responsibilities. If the contractor is on board at this point in the process, whether involved through single-stage design and build or two-stage tendering, is it important that the project lead protects the detailed coordination activities of the design team rather than being pressured into accepting a package mentality by the contractor, who will be intent on obtaining cost certainty by early procurement of the information in package format. Designing elements as packages requires a clear understanding of the interfaces between the various elements of design, which become harder to identify if the designers are concentrating on content by package rather than component. The natural process of design requires that a greater level of resolution is achieved before entering into design by package to ensure that nothing slips between the packages and that no discrepancies arise due to information being developed in silos.

During this stage, the BIM model is central to the coordination activities, as further layers of detail are added to the model, initiating regular conversations between design team members to detect clashes and coordinate the design information. It will be important for the project lead to properly discuss and agree the format of information to be issued to contractors for pricing, whether it be in traditional 2D format or whether the BIM model contains an appropriate level of information for the contractors to cost accurately. More complex buildings will use a combination of both information types.

What are the Core Objectives of this stage?

The Core Objectives of the RIBA Plan of Work 2013 at Stage 4 are:

Tasks ▼	**4** Technical Design
Core Objectives	Prepare **Technical Design** in accordance with **Design Responsibility Matrix** and **Project Strategies** to include all architectural, structural and building services information, specialist subcontractor design and specifications, in accordance with **Design Programme**.

Technical Design as part of a traditional single-stage contract has now become the final pre-contract stage for the design team. However, this is not the whole story as procurement is no longer prescriptive in the 2013 Plan of Work; the contractor could already be on board at this stage and, even if not, subcontractor design is also commonly introduced into this stage. As mentioned above, potential problems occur when a clear period of time for detailed coordination is no longer safeguarded or separated from the procurement process. Prices sought from the contractor's supply chain and fixed prior to this critical activity may be subject to variation as the opportunity to take a closer look at the design interfaces is at risk of being overlooked due to the pressures on the design team to enter into the production of both the tender and contract information.

The design principles in general terms should be frozen by the end of Stage 3; Stage 4 is therefore about focusing on the detailing and detailed coordination between the architecture, the core engineering disciplines, the specialist consultants and potential for design work by the specialist subcontractors. It will also involve the creation of a contract set of drawings suitable for entering into a contract with a building contractor.

How contractor's designed portions affect the work of the design team

Contractor's designed portions are a subset of the design work undertaken by specialist contractors on all forms of contract, as defined within the Design Responsibility Matrix, and need to be identified prior to the commencement of the Technical Design stage to ensure that the design team understands the extent of the detail to be incorporated within the design information to be produced. This is to avoid the risk of variance in the extent of contractor design responsibilities relative to the extent of the consultant design duties. There is no point in preparing a fully prescriptive set of drawings if the contractor has been asked to take full responsibility for the design. The contractor's development of these areas of the building will almost certainly supersede any detailed design work carried out by the design team.

Technical Design activities

Technical Design can be carried out as part of the design team's direct appointment with the client if the preferred procurement route is established earlier in the process as a standard traditional lump sum contract. Alternatively, the contractor could already be appointed at this stage, with the design team working in collaboration with the contractor to develop the final information required to be able to comprehensively price and build the project. The impact of procurement on this stage is described later in this chapter.

Technical Design will generally move up another scale from the work completed during Developed Design. The systems specified will be interrogated at a greater level of detail to ensure the design is now fully coordinated so that procurement and construction can take place with confidence that post-contract amendments can be kept to a minimum.

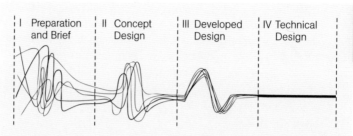

Figure 4.1   Aligning the design activities at Technical Design

During Technical Design the drawings will include larger scale drawings for specific areas of the design. These larger scale drawings (1:20 or 1:50) will be cross-referenced to construction details at a scale of 1:10 or 1:5. (If BIM is being used then scale is less of an issue other than to inform the level of detail anticipated within the BIM model at a particular stage.) As mentioned above, it is important for the project lead to agree with the lead designer which packages will be contractor design, to make sure that the design team concentrates on communicating the design intent rather than prescriptive construction detailing that is likely to be superseded, or at the least duplicated, by the information to be provided by the contractor.

The diagram in figure 4.1 provides a clear indication of the level of alignment between the core consultants as the design activities progress. The objective at this stage of the design is to collate a complete set of design documentation that adequately describes the project and that the information from every participating project team member is properly integrated.

On larger, more complex projects this informal approach should be supplemented with regular formal design team meetings. These design

Small projects at Stage 4

On small projects, design integration can be very informal with meetings between different disciplines taking place as and when required. These meetings should be used to deal with specific design issues that cannot be addressed by telephone or email.

team meetings allow issues to be discussed between all team members and, once a coordinated approach is adopted, will be the main method by which design coordination is achieved.

In the case of both traditional and design-and-build contracts, the Technical Design stage is critical to the success of the project and requires an in-depth review of the building components, services and external works. All elements of the design must be properly tested and approved at Stage 4 so that changes do not occur during construction.

Once the project lead is confident that the requisite level of Technical Design details have been produced and that comprehensive integration has taken place, the design team will commence working on producing construction drawings and on developing the specifications, so the contractor will be able to market test the construction costs and subsequently build the project.

These construction drawings and specifications are prepared in order to define in detail all of the materials that are to be used in the project and where they are to be located, as well as how they are to be installed. These drawings and specifications become part of the construction contract.

Although this phase is primarily intended to work out the technical aspects of the project, some final design work will also take place, sometimes in collaboration with the contractor's supply chain. During this stage, some lower cost items, such as fit-out items and finishes materials that may have been subject to provisional sums, are selected with the client. Finally, the project lead must facilitate the final client review of the project prior to issue of tender documentation.

Now that the design has been developed to a sufficient level of documented detail, the project lead will need to instigate robust interrogation of the design from a buildability and logistics perspective to help test the final solutions with the contractor. The pros and cons of various construction methodologies can be properly reviewed, coordinating the input of cost, operational and production implications of the design proposals.

This is the last opportunity to ensure that the design has properly considered the site constraints, local authority guidelines and real practicalities of production, time, access, safety and all issues relating to value and efficiency in the construction process.

As part of the work during Technical Design, a full specification will be required to support the drawn documentation; specifications are discussed in more detail below.

Design Programme

The production of design information during Technical Design naturally becomes more linear than in the previous stages. The scale and frequency of the design iterations reduce as the information becomes more detailed and increases significantly in terms of volume. The Design Programme at this stage can be more prescriptive and can identify in far more detail the information to be produced and also project reasonably accurate timescales onto the documentation. It is therefore more appropriate to apply a Gantt chart to this stage than a Plan of Work style approach.

The Technical Design Programme will provide an overview of the key activities, their durations and the interrelationships with other activities in order to give the client and design team an understanding of the overall time line. It will also have been used to help shape the overall timescale of the project and then, with further input from the project team, it will be refined and developed to a working document that all parties can access and use.

The more detailed stage Design Programmes will need to be developed from the Project Programme, considering the detail of design activities, package procurement milestones and anticipated construction/procurement milestones, to help the design team to understand the context of the procurement activities. These detailed programmes allow the project team to appreciate the interrelationship between each other's activities – especially important during the Technical Design stage where the coordinated design is being translated into Technical Design information.

Detailed specifications

Specifications are the written requirements for a material or product for a proposed project. The detailed specifications will form part of the activities during Technical Design and will be wholly coordinated and cross-referenced with the drawings.

The intent of the specifications should be communicated by the project lead and agreed with the lead designer and the design team. The project

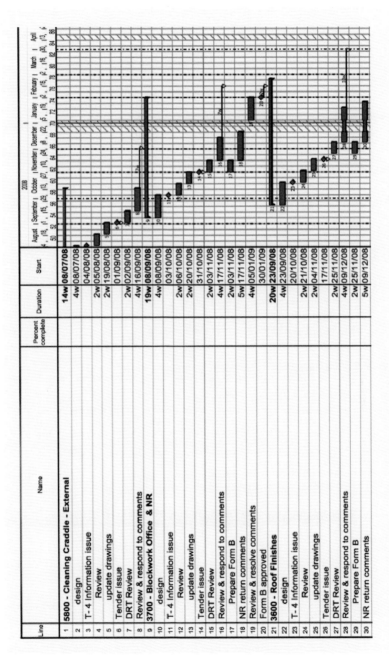

Figure 4.2 Example of a Technical Design Programme

lead should ensure that all parties understand the objectives of the specifications and make sure these are appropriate to the form of Building Contract being proposed. The following is a guide to the purposes behind specifications:

I Specifications should describe the type and quality of every product required for the project.
I The specifications should describe the requirements for fabrication, erection, application, installation and finishing.
I Specifications should describe the quality of workmanship necessary for the project. This includes all phases of creation and installation, starting with manufacturing, fabrication and application, through installation to finishing and adjustment.
I Specifications should include any necessary codes and standards applicable to the project.
I The specifications should also include descriptions and procedures for alternative materials, products or services, if necessary.
I The contractor's responsibilities with respect to prescriptive and descriptive elements of the works should be detailed in the specifications.
I The specifications define the requirements for submittals, including pre/post-tender samples, mock-ups, prototypes and quality benchmarks.

There are three main methods of specifying, with no clear rules for using one method over another or combining methods, but care should be taken to avoid the inclusion of irrelevant or conflicting information. The three methods are:

I prescriptive
I descriptive
I performance.

Prescriptive specifications

Under this method the design team has design responsibility and the contractor carries out the works in accordance with the drawings and specification. This approach presupposes that the design team knows exactly what it wants, has worked out exactly how it should be done and is allowed by relevant legislation to specify manufacturers and suppliers.

Within prescriptive specifications, it is normal to highlight the proposed manufacturer or supplier with the understanding that the contractor may propose an 'acceptable equivalent' alternative that also meets the requirements of the client.

Advantages:

I single point of design responsibility (with the design team), minimising potential conflict
I cost consultants are often more comfortable with 'known' information.

Disadvantages:

I design responsibility rests with the design team
I design must be sufficiently developed to allow a system to be prescribed
I limits the contractor's opportunities to bring their expertise to the design solution.

Descriptive specifications

Under this method, the properties of the materials and methods of installation are described in detail without using proprietary or manufacturers' names. The specification may include indicative manufacturers with the caveat that acceptable equivalents will also be satisfactory. Descriptive specifications are commonly used in situations where the design team needs to exercise tight control over the specified work.

Advantages:

I descriptive specifications specify exactly what the design intends
I they can be applied to all conditions, methods or situations of a project
I they are applicable to all project scales and project types
I they permit open competition because they do not restrict the contractor to the use of specific products or manufacturers.

Disadvantages:

I they require the specifier to take special care in describing the design intent in order to achieve the desired results

I they tend to be more extensive because they require more technical detail than other methods

I they may be more time consuming than other methods to create and write

I they are being used less often as more complete reference standards are being developed and implemented.

Performance specifications

Under this method the required end results are specified along with the criteria by which the performance will be judged and the method by which it can be validated. The contractor is free to choose the materials and methods that comply with the performance specification. They are generally used to encourage the use of new and innovative techniques that may lead to more economical and efficient construction.

Advantages:

I only the end result or design intent is specified, allowing the contractor flexibility in selecting and applying products

I they permit open competition

I they can be applicable to all types and sizes of projects

I performance specifications delegate the technical responsibilities to the contractor and the contractor's supply chain, where the contractor rather than the design team is responsible for the design.

Disadvantages:

I they can be time consuming to produce and may result in long, detailed specifications

I they are more difficult to enforce than other methods of specifying

I they may be too elaborate for simple or minor projects

I performance specifications delegate the technical responsibilities to the contractor and the contractor's supply chain, where the contractor rather than the design team is responsible for the design and therefore there is little or no control over the visual aspect of the proposal.

Do not underestimate the importance of a coordinated specification

The art of specification writing is diminishing within many architecture practices and specialist specification writers are becoming the norm on the larger, more complex projects. The specification is one of the most important documents both for establishing an accurate price from the contractor and for the construction works as a whole. It describes aspects of quality that cannot be included on the drawings and requires accurate cross-referencing with the drawings to provide a more complete picture of the design.

Discharge of planning conditions

On receipt of the planning permission (the application will have been submitted at the end of Stage 3, or possibly Stage 2), it is usual for the local planning authority to have applied conditions to the consent; these are called 'reserved matters' and will have various time limits by which they must be discharged. The project lead will have to identify which conditions require submission of further details or information and the dates by which compliance is necessary. Some conditions must be complied with before a development is started, some regulate how the work is undertaken, others require actions to be completed before the development is occupied or a use commences, while certain conditions will seek to regulate how the completed development is to be used or control possible changes in the future. The project lead will need to assess, in consultation with any appointed advisers, how best to comply with those conditions. It is advisable that a planning conditions tracker (see figure 4.3) is prepared, which logs all reserved matters, the timeframe within which they require approval and the owner of the activities that support their resolution. Please refer to *RIBA Plan of Work 2013 Guide: Town Planning* in this series, which covers the planning process in more detail.

Contract documents

The content of the Building Contract documentation generally responds to the type of contract that is being entered into by the client and may or may not be earlier in the process. In a single-stage traditional form of

Town Planning Conditions Tracker

Project Name

Issue No: 1
Date: 07/12/2011

P1 – Critical
P2 – High
P3 – Medium

Urgent/prompt action required
Action required
Agree/completed

Planning Reference	Condition	Action Owner	Action Required	Priority	RAG	Action Required By (date)	Action Progress Review Date	Status	Comments/Notes

Figure 4.3 Planning conditions tracker

contract, the design team will provide all the necessary information for the contractor to construct the works unless contractor's designed portions have been identified within the contract. This allows the final detailed design to be developed by the contractor's supply chain in accordance with the design intent drawings provided by the design team. This places design responsibility into the hands of those best placed to understand the technicalities of complex systems, such as facades or some MEP items.

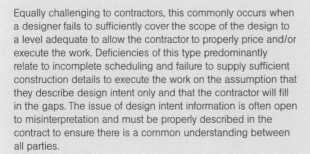

Providing insufficient design information

Equally challenging to contractors, this commonly occurs when a designer fails to sufficiently cover the scope of the design to a level adequate to allow the contractor to properly price and/or execute the work. Deficiencies of this type predominantly relate to incomplete scheduling and failure to supply sufficient construction details to execute the work on the assumption that they describe design intent only and that the contractor will fill in the gaps. The issue of design intent information is often open to misinterpretation and must be properly described in the contract to ensure there is a common understanding between all parties.

In the case of design and build contracts, the design information provided by the design team takes the form of Employer's Requirements. This set of information recognises the fact that the contractor has the ability to develop (in collaboration with in-house or consultant designers appointed by them) the design intent information provided by the design team. The information provided is therefore incomplete in terms of its technical content, but rather concentrates on the design intent for particular elements of the design. Design intent is the term used to describe information that outlines the visual and aesthetic aspects of the design. The design team accepts that the contractor will develop the detailed design in accordance with a performance specification which defines the technical criteria of the element or system proposed.

As part of the tendering process, and in order to be in a better position to propose a guaranteed lump sum price with confidence, the design and build contractor will respond to this information by developing a set of Contractor's Proposals. These will, to a certain extent, attempt to fill in the gaps in the Employer's Requirements by proposing detailed solutions that reflect the design intent information provided by the design team as part of the Employer's Requirements. In adopting the risk associated with the design responsibility, the contractor under a design and build contract has the option of proposing alternative solutions that may yield advantages in terms of either time or cost savings, or both. However, this is only permissible on the basis that the alternative proposals comply with both the performance criteria contained within the specifications and the aesthetic principles outlined in the design intent documentation.

The design team needs to assess the Contractor's Proposals carefully as, in certain situations, they could potentially supersede the Employer's Requirements. Under the JCT Design and Build Contract, an unresolved problem occurs when there is a discrepancy between the Employer's Requirements and the Contractor's Proposals.

Design discrepancy

The Employer's Requirements may specify a particular manufacturer for ironmongery, whereas the Contractor's Proposals include an alternative proposal and, although both are generally fit for purpose, there remains a discrepancy. A clause in the JCT Design and Build Contract appears to align with the contractor's view that their alternative solution is acceptable under the contract, in that: *'The Employer has examined the Contractor's Proposals and, subject to the Conditions, is satisfied that they appear to meet the Employer's Requirements.'*

The original intention in the emergence of design and build contracts is that the contractor both completes the designs and then builds to them. Employer's Requirements are meant to be descriptive rather than prescriptive, allowing the contractor to develop and configure the design to achieve broadly stated rather than strictly defined aims. However, clients, their advisers and their designers often attempt to define the design to inappropriately prescriptive levels prior to the contract being signed, while imposing on the contractor all liability for that design, in which the contractor has not participated. This needs to be appreciated in a considered way by the design team while reviewing and approving the contractor's alternative proposals.

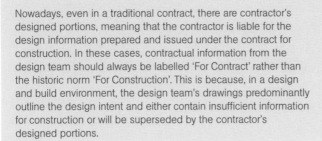

Labelling of contract documents

Nowadays, even in a traditional contract, there are contractor's designed portions, meaning that the contractor is liable for the design information prepared and issued under the contract for construction. In these cases, contractual information from the design team should always be labelled 'For Contract' rather than the historic norm 'For Construction'. This is because, in a design and build environment, the design team's drawings predominantly outline the design intent and either contain insufficient information for construction or will be superseded by the contractor's designed portions.

Package definition

As discussed earlier in this chapter, the emphasis during Stage 4 from a design team perspective should be on the development of detailed design information and its final integration prior to issue to the contractor for construction. It is imperative that the project lead recognises the importance of these activities and protects the quality and integrity of the design by resisting the pressure that will inevitably be applied by the contractor to enter 'package procurement mode'.

Packaging up information to suit a contractor's procurement activities must occur once the design has been developed to an appropriate level of detail (which is dependent on who owns the design responsibility) and has been through a thorough coordination exercise or, in the case of integrated BIM techniques, a full clash detection exercise. Package definition will generally be dictated by the contractor, in a manner which suits their need to achieve cost certainty as early as possible in the procurement of the systems and materials specified for the building.

Fully coordinated detailed design cannot be easily achieved following this methodology because a package approach, by its very nature, does not fully consider the interfaces and dependencies of the design. It is the interfaces between packages that present the greatest challenge to the different disciplines of the design team in the successful coordination of the detailed works. For example, to the designer the transition between floors, walls and ceilings needs to be considered and developed holistically

Ensure that the design interfaces are clearly understood

A useful tool to ensure that all relationships between the various packages and materials are identified and addressed is to schedule out a design interface matrix of all the adjacent systems and materials that have the potential to affect the proposals. These can generally be found at the junctions of floors to walls and walls to ceilings/roofs but can also be defined as the influence of later works on earlier works, such as finished floor drainage on structural slabs and distribution of fit-out services on hidden structures. Understanding these interfaces means that there are likely to be fewer surprises in the definition of the design and its coordination.

to make sure that all adjacent elements are considered in context rather than in isolation.

Impact of procurement on technical design activities

The activities in Stage 4 Technical Design will vary depending on the procurement strategy established earlier in the process. The three most common methods of procurement and their impact on the Stage 4 activities are described below:

Procurement strategies

Single-stage traditional tender
If this route is followed, the objective at the end of Stage 4 is to provide sufficient design information that adequately describes all aspects of the project to allow tendering contractors to price the project accurately and, ultimately, use the design team's documentation to construct the development. This requires all drawings or 3D models to be prepared to a significant level of detail. They will have to be fully coordinated across all disciplines and supported by schedules, specifications and samples.

Procurement strategies (*continued*)

The exception to this is where pre-agreed contractor's designed portions (CDPs) are to be included within the traditional contract documentation, as described within the Design Responsibility Matrix. This situation recognises the fact that expertise in certain areas of the design may lie outside the capabilities of the design team and sit with specialist subcontractors. In this case, the design team documentation in respect of these packages describes the design intent only, supported by a performance specification for the specialist subcontractor to complete the design using their specialist knowledge of the systems to be procured. Design intent essentially identifies the profiles required from a visual perspective, the technical details will be provided by the specialist subcontractor and the responsibility for the design and performance will lie with the contractor.

For projects based on partial contractor design, the demarcation of responsibility is far more critical. There are two aspects that need to be considered in this regard:

1. Clear communication of the extent of design responsibility allocated to the contractor, making sure that designers stay strictly within the boundaries of their scope of work.
2. Continuing coordination of the work of the contractor and their specialists, as contractor-designed work is integrated into the client's design solution.

Single-stage design and build

In the situation where the client prefers that the contractor takes full responsibility for the complete design, the project costs and the programme, then a design and build contract is the most common route to achieve this. The design and build contractor is usually procured on the basis of the Stage 3 design information or the Employer's Requirements and therefore they will be appointed on the basis of a fixed lump sum price. This will include a fee for completing the design during Stage 4, and needs to include adequate time to complete the design and coordination process.

The contractor can complete the design in one of two ways: either by using the skills and resources of a separate design team appointed by and reporting to the contractor (this could be an internal team retained by the contractor) or by transferring and adopting the appointment of the incumbent design team from the client. This process is called novation and requires the core members of the design team to complete the design activities

Procurement strategies (*continued*)

under contract to the contractor in collaboration with the supply chain. One of the advantages of this is the early engagement of specialist subcontractors prior to the completion of the design documentation, providing beneficial and expert input into the design earlier in the process. In a design and build contract, the contractor has the opportunity to propose alternative solutions that meet the design intent and performance criteria of the Employer's Requirements. Under appointment to the contractor, the design team will have less influence over the acceptability of these amendments from a purely aesthetic perspective than if its appointment was retained by the client.

Two-stage design and build

Two-stage design and build has similar characteristics to single-stage design and build but, as the name suggests, the selection and appointment of the contractor is carried out over two stages. The first stage usually requires prequalification (to ensure that first-stage tenderers meet the minimum requirements of the client in terms of experience, financial stability and quality of precedent projects) prior to a submission of fixed costs for preliminaries, overheads and profit in addition to the pre-contract services for Stage 2 of the process.

The novated design team, in collaboration with the contractor, develops the Developed Design to a detailed Technical Design and complete set of working drawings that respond to the Employer's Requirements. The client and their retained advisers (which could include the project lead) will review the Contractor's Proposals against the Stage 3 cost plan, the further design work is completed, and any remaining design development uncertainty is resolved. If the client and their advisers determine that the Contractor's Proposals are acceptable, the Building Contract is entered into. Depending on the circumstances, the incumbent design team can be novated to the contractor to carry out any remaining design development. Alternatively, the design team may oversee further design work by design consultants engaged by the contractor as outlined in the description of single-stage tendering above.

The contractor may begin enabling works and work on early packages but in such a way that, should the second-stage contract negotiation fail, the works can be handed over to an alternative contractor. If the second-stage negotiation does fail, the Building Contract can be tendered and an alternative contractor can be appointed.

During the second stage of a two-stage procurement route, whether the design team is novated or retained by the client as design quality monitors, the project lead may retain their appointment by the client to ensure impartiality and consistency in the oversight and direction of the project. In this case their role would switch from that of design team leader to one of employer representative, ensuring that the client's interests are protected during this contractor-led stage of the Building Contract.

Samples procurement – mock-up definition

It is important for the project lead to extract from the lead designer and the design team the level of prototyping, mock-ups and samples required to demonstrate both the technical performance and the visual qualities of a particular installation or material. The timing and procurement of these vary depending on the relative importance to the design and the level of innovation anticipated in the manufacture of the component. Samples will be obtained throughout the design process as the design team selects and reviews materials. These are generally obtained directly from the supplier as and when required throughout the early stage of design.

With ever-more innovative and unique building design comes the need to ensure the performance of external structural and aesthetic facade and curtain wall technology. Specialist facilities can accommodate facades of many sizes and design types. The testing requirement can be used for design validation at the pre-construction phase or on site, as part of the quality assurance/quality control programme. This testing demonstrates to the client (and to the design team) both the aesthetic and the technical qualities of the proposals and usually takes the form of two different kinds of mock-up – visual and technical. The cost of these can be significant and usually it is the larger, higher profile projects that will require this level of design justification.

Technical mock-ups

Technical mock-ups are used to test the weather integrity of the proposals when a facade system has been proposed without existing testing criteria in place. A portion of the facade would be identified that contains typically awkward junctions that may be vulnerable when subjected to prolonged exposure to the elements. An actual representation of this area of the facade would be constructed to replicate the technical detailing proposed; the mock-up would then be subjected to a variety of tests. The project lead will need to ensure that the design team or specialist facade consultant specifies the appropriate level of testing to demonstrate compliance with the relevant standards prior to committing to the procurement of the entire facade. This testing can include the following performance criteria: wind load pressure, water penetration tests, climatic studies, energy transmission and seismic and thermal considerations.

Visual mock-ups

Visual mock-ups are also useful in helping the design team and the client visualise the drawn proposals before committing to the procurement of the components or materials. In the case of facades, the visual mock-ups can be constructed in a way that mimics the design rather than necessarily being an accurate representation, as no performance testing is required with these mock-ups.

Benchmarking samples

Benchmarking samples are essential as part of the specification of the works. These samples need to be requested of every specialist subcontractor in the tender documentation and are necessary to ensure that a common understanding of a particular visual range of mostly natural materials is achieved. The process considers the boundaries of texture, colour and naturally occurring flaws in any material and will help to avoid disputes during the installation.

Pre-tender estimate

At this stage of the design in traditional procurement, it is usual for the cost consultant to prepare a pre-tender estimate. The pre-tender estimate will, at this stage, respond to the design documentation and will be measured from drawings, schedules and specifications and therefore will be an accurate representation of the design information available. Information that is to be developed at a later stage can be the subject of provisional sums or prime cost sums.

Provisional sums

Provisional sums are generally used as place-markers to ensure that there is sufficient allowance within the Building Contract for installations where the design information available is insufficient to properly price the works or there is a degree of uncertainty as to whether the installation will be incorporated or not. There will have to be spatial provision within the design to allow these areas of the design to be incorporated at a later date without impacting the overall coordination of the proposals.

Prime cost sums (PC sums)

In construction, the term PC sum is often confused with a provisional sum. Although both terms are associated with certain allowances being made for a specific activity or item, there are distinct differences in their definition. PC sums are normally associated with an average cost of a specific item whereas provisional sums are generally estimated allowances. The PC sum should reflect the material allowance being made in the rate for a specific item. A quoted rate will normally consist of material, labour, plant and profit and overheads.

The use of PC sums is very popular in the domestic market as clients with limited building knowledge understand this concept and enjoy having control over the selection process for materials during the later construction stages of the project.

The pre-tender estimate is ultimately used as a point of reference in the analysis of contractors' tender returns. There should only be a minimal divergence between the pre-tender estimate and the mean of the contractors' commercial tender submissions.

Tender documentation – key content

The information to be prepared for a single-stage traditional tender must be properly defined by the project lead and will generally take the form of the following:

Typical tender documentation

- Form of tender
- Terms and conditions of the Building Contract
- Bills of quantities
- Design documentation
- Specifications
- Required methodologies and supporting information
- Selection criteria
- Pre-construction information (health and safety)
- Project Programme

Form of tender

The form of tender is generally issued as a covering document prepared by the project lead to be signed and returned by each tenderer to confirm that they understand the tender and accept the various terms and conditions of the contract and all other requirements described in the tender documentation.

Terms and conditions

This document sets out the legal conditions of both the client and the contractor who are signing up to the contract. It sets out procedure and conditions and should be read in conjunction with the other tender documents.

Some terms and conditions can be very lengthy and complex, but will be necessary for larger, more complex projects where the risk can be significant for the parties involved.

Bills of quantities

Although becoming less common, bills of quantities are used as the description and quantities of all aspects of the project, allowing the contractor to enter their anticipated prices for carrying out all works. The bill of quantities assists tendering contractors in the production of an estimate of the construction costs and provides a level playing field ensuring that all contractors are using the same quantities, rather than risking misinterpretation of the quantities taken off by each contractor from the construction documentation. A similar document that schedules out the work but without quantities is called a pricing schedule.

Each contractor tendering for the project is able to price the work on exactly the same information with a minimum of effort. This therefore avoids duplication in quantifying the work, and allows for the fairest type of competition. The bill of quantities also provides a valuable aid to the pricing of variations and computation of valuations for interim certificates.

Design documentation

This includes clear and comprehensive detailed documents about the construction site and the building's design. They are the essential ingredients for informing tenderers of exactly what is required to complete all works. The documentation must be cross-referenced to the specification, fully dimensioned, set out to pre-agreed datums and fully annotated.

Specifications

Specifications set out policies, procedures or guidelines to be followed. They set out the performance criteria and the quality aspects of the outcomes expected. They describe the materials and workmanship standards. They must be read alongside other tender documentation, such as the terms and conditions of the contract, bills of quantities and the construction drawings. They do not include cost, quantity or drawn information and will have been described in more detail in Stage 4.

Required methodologies and supporting information

A questionnaire about how the contractor intends to provide the contracting service, including supporting evidence demonstrating relevant experience will be used to help evaluate the quality of the bid.

Further supporting information will be requested of the contractor. This will typically include:

I Construction Programme
I methodologies
I resource projections
I insurances
I legal ownership documents
I collateral warranties
I parent company guarantees
I quality plans
I equality policy
I handover and close out procedure.

Selection criteria

This document advises how the tender submitted will be evaluated and the contract awarded.

Pre-construction information

The pre-construction information, which the client must provide for all construction projects (but which is a legal requirement for notifiable projects only) should contain all the relevant information in the client's possession, or which they can easily obtain, about the construction project that might affect health and safety aspects of design and construction work.

Project Programme

The Project Programme will be included within the tender documentation to ensure the contractor complies with the timescale objectives of the client.

Tenderers must follow the instructions and information given in each tender document provided, as failure to do so may make the submission null and void.

Tender reviews

During the tender review process, the project lead should aim to achieve value for money in the procurement of the main contractor. This procedure benefits from clear project definition and selection of the most appropriate procurement method for the project.

The tendering process aims to ensure that the most suitable contractor is selected for the project. Traditionally, many construction contracts have been awarded to the company with the lowest priced conforming tender. However, this practice clearly values price above competence and there will be many occasions when this method will not result in the selection of the most suitable contractor for the project. In these situations, a more appropriate tender evaluation process using weighted criteria can be adopted to determine the tender that offers the best value. This process is utilised where the performance of the contractor is of crucial importance to achieving the required outcome.

The weighted criteria method of tender evaluation requires that selection criteria in addition to price are included in tender returns and form part of the tender assessment process. A system of weighting the selection criteria is used to compare tenders and identify the tenderer with the best performance record in terms of time, cost and value for money.

All relevant information requested in the tender documents and provided with the tender is used in the tender evaluation.

Appropriate selection criteria are required to assess the competence of the contractors in order to assess their ability to achieve the required project outcome and are used to rate each of the tenders.

Selection criteria

The criteria are usually selected from the following:

- relevant experience
- understanding of the project
- demonstrable performance
- available references
- management and technical capabilities
- proposed resources and personalities
- management processes
- construction methodology
- cost
- programme.

Generally, no more than five of the above criteria would be used. The criteria must be relevant to the project, they must be able to be evaluated in a meaningful and consistent manner and they should be able to be used to allocate a score to each of the tender submissions.

A tender report should be prepared on all tenders received. The report should address the selection criteria for all tenders and allow the project lead to make an unqualified recommendation on the preferred contractor.

Contractor design submittals

Following appointment, the contractor will be required to submit further detailed design information in respect of contractor design submittals to the design team for review and approval. This will have to take place whether the design team is novated or not and the project lead must ensure that all disciplines within the design team understand the levels and timescales of commitment required to review the information in respect of compliance with the design intent contained within the Employer's Requirements.

As part of the first stage appointment with the contractor, the project lead will, in conjunction with the other design team members, have to agree with the contractor the process for the submission of drawings, technical submissions, samples and mock-ups by the contractor.

The design team will receive, review and comment on the contractor's designers' drawings, technical submissions, samples and mock-ups that have been submitted. The lead designer for the particular element of design will coordinate the comments of other designers, mark up one set of coordinated comments and agree the status with the project lead as follows:

1. 'Status A' – the submittal has no comments: the contractor may proceed.
2. 'Status B Proceed with comments' – the contractor must comply with the comments and amend information accordingly prior to proceeding with the works, but may proceed without resubmitting the information for approval unless they identify additional consequences arising from the amendment.
3. 'Status C Rejected' – the contractor must not proceed with the works, but must rework the submittal and make a resubmission to achieve Status A or B before proceeding.

The set of coordinated comments will be returned to the contractor and distributed within the design team according to the agreed process. Any approvals issued by the design team will not remove the design liability for the design work of the contractor.

Resubmission of Status B documentation

The project lead must make sure that the contractor follows up on Status B shop drawings returned to the contractor. The concentration of effort by the contractor on the resolution of Status C drawings tends to be prioritised to allow information to be released to the supply chain for manufacture. Status B allows the contractor to progress, conditional on the integration of design team comments into the proposals – this often happens without formal update and resubmission of the design information and needs to be monitored to ensure that the consolidated and final design information is produced and held as a record of what is being procured and constructed.

Tendering

The tendering process is covered in more detail in *RIBA Plan of Work 2013 Guide: Contract Administration* in this series.

Construction Strategy

The Construction Strategy document is generally prepared by the contractor and sets out the intent for the construction of the project and associated infrastructure. The Construction Strategy does not set out to provide specific details on the methods to be employed in construction or the specific legislation with which the contractor must comply, but it will provide the project lead with a chance to assess whether the contractor is keeping abreast of current construction methodologies and whether they are at the leading edge of innovation and industry best practice.

The Construction Strategy will outline the approach that the contractor will take during the construction works. It is not so much about the detailed technical construction techniques but concerns more the management of the site and the disruptive activities to neighbours and others arising from the construction process.

The Construction Strategy will include the following content as a minimum; this is again dependent on the scale and complexity of the project:

Construction Strategy

1. Construction methodologies
   a. Demolition
   b. Substructure
   c. Superstructure
   d. Infrastructure
2. Construction sequencing including phasing, decanting and temporary accommodation
3. Contractor's welfare and management facilities, canteen, medical room, security etc.

Construction Strategy (*continued*)

4. Mitigation of impact of construction activities
   a. On neighbours (businesses and residents)
   b. On highways/traffic
   c. On the environment (protected trees)
   d. From dust
   e. From construction noise
   f. Wheel washing, street cleansing
5. Logistics and deliveries, including types, times and controls
6. Distribution of site materials (fork lift, tower cranes, hoists, other)
7. Surface water management plan

Chapter summary   4

Stage 4 recognises the variable activities resulting from alternative procurement strategies and the potential for the contractor to be appointed at the commencement of this stage. While there are tangible benefits from early contractor involvement, there are also issues that arise from the impact of the project leadership transferring to the contractor at this stage. Unless they have been involved from the start of the design process, the contractor's objectives prior to the commencement of site activities will not necessarily align with those of the client or the design team. Protection of the critical coordination work and the completion of a robust and appropriately detailed design or design intent is essential and must be safeguarded by the project lead prior to the transfer of this role to the contractor.

The issue of design quality also arises at this stage as the contractor focuses on achieving certainty of both cost and buildability at the potential expense of the coordination and production of the final design information. Coordination problems on site will be disproportionate in terms of time and cost compared to those resolved on paper as part of the final design stage for the design team. Whichever procurement route is selected, the only way to protect design quality is to ensure that it is properly defined in the tender and subsequent construction documentation.

Construction

Chapter Overview

Stage 5 comprises contractor mobilisation and construction activities. This stage will encompass offsite manufacturing and onsite Construction in accordance with the Construction Programme and resolution of Design Queries from site as they arise. The role of contract administrator under various contracts will also commence at this stage, providing impartial administration of the Building Contract on behalf of the client.

The key coverage in this chapter is as follows:

Core Objectives

Project lead roles during Construction

Construction Programme

Offsite construction

Health and Safety Strategy during Construction

Handover Strategy

Soft Landings

Defining Practical Completion

Zero defects

'As-constructed' Information

Introduction

Stage 5 Construction is not simply about construction activities but also includes mobilisation and the final resolution of potential contractor's designed portions, which will have commenced during Stage 4 and commonly overlap with the commencement of Construction. There is also potential for contractor activities to be advanced prior to entering into a main contract, such as demolition, enabling works, services diversions, utilities capacity enhancements and even separate foundation, substructure contracts or offsite production. These activities all have the potential advantage of reducing the overall Project Programme but need careful definition and management if they are to run parallel to the Stage 4 Technical Design development.

A significant level of discipline is also required to ensure that the information that informs the following packages is frozen, so the early contracts will essentially become a fixed constraint to the developing design information for the main tender. During the construction phase the party undertaking the project lead role could be undertaking various roles and responsibilities, not least that of contract administrator, employer's agent, design quality monitor etc. This chapter will explain the various roles and activities during the construction stage that will require active management by the project lead, or consideration as to who is best placed to undertake them in different circumstances.

What are the Core Objectives of this stage?

The Core Objectives of the RIBA Plan of Work 2013 at Stage 5 are:

Tasks ▼	**5** Construction
Core Objectives	Offsite manufacturing and onsite **Construction** in accordance with **Construction Programme** and resolution of **Design Queries** from site as they arise.

Once the contractor has been appointed, they will commence the mobilisation stage and, if not already working alongside existing pre-contract appointments, will start the process of appointing subcontractors for the first stage of construction and commencing site set-up. Following the signing of the Building Contract, the contractor will need time to allocate people, material and machinery. This period between the contract signing and the date of actual commencement of the work is called 'mobilisation' and is an important period for the contractor, the client and the project lead. During this period, the contractor will comprehensively plan out the works in accordance with the Construction Programme contained within the Building Contract. During the construction phase, the main contractor is responsible for the planning and execution of the works but, alongside this, many activities will continue to be the responsibility of the project lead or the contract administrator.

At the earliest opportunity, the project lead will have to ensure that the Building Contract documents are prepared, agreed and signed off and that any performance bonds and/or collateral warranties are in place. There will be documentation, methodologies and processes requested as part of the Building Contract that will have to be provided by the contractor and the project lead will need to check that these have been submitted. Relevant personnel will have to be formally advised of the commencement of works prior to the site being handed over to the contractor.

Project lead roles during Construction

At the commencement of the construction stage of the project, the project lead's role can take one of several changes in direction by adopting one of the following roles:

I contract administrator
I employer's representative/agent
I design quality monitor
I novated lead designer.

Essentially, this leadership role, regardless of how it is contracted, maintains the objectives of ensuring that the contractor is following the requirements of the Building Contract and the contract documentation.

Project lead roles

Contract administrator
Depending on the contract in use, the contract administrator (CA) has a formal role in managing the Building Contract between the employer and the contractor. The role of CA has been in existence on building projects for centuries, although the term was only formally defined in the JCT form of contract in 1987.

This is a role that was traditionally performed by the architect or lead designer; in fact, the JCT form refers to 'architect/contract administrator', indicating that for the purpose of the role identified there is no contractual difference between the two terms. The CA makes sure that all parties employ due diligence to comply with the terms, conditions, rights and obligations of the Building Contract. They will also coordinate any changes to the agreement

Project lead roles (*continued*)

that might occur over the course of the contract and perform the close-out process when both parties have met their obligations. There is usually no requirement for an impartial CA in design and build contracts.

Employer's representative/agent

For the purposes of this chapter, the role is as defined in the JCT Design and Build Contract and is different to the role of CA as the obligation is to act exclusively for the client (the employer). This involves providing input and responses to the contractor and the CA on behalf of the client. The employer's agent role involves obtaining advice on the quality, cost and programme of the works, making recommendations for interim payments and facilitating agreement of the final account. They will liaise with all members of the project team and prepare and maintain both the handover plan and the defects administration plan.

Design quality monitor

The role of the design quality monitor is to make sure that the building project is realised as specified, within the agreed limits of time, costs, scope and quality. This role is procured by the client when they have entered into a design and build contract to provide expert advice on whether the works are being executed in accordance with the Building Contract documentation. This requires a detailed understanding of the design parameters, acting as the client's eyes and ears on site when the design team has been novated.

Novated lead designer

During design and build contracts, the responsibility for the detailed design sits with the contractor. The provision of detailed design services is therefore also the responsibility of the contractor, who will separately employ the services of core designers as part of the team. Alternatively, the incumbent design team may be novated to the contractor under a pre-agreed scope of services to fulfil the obligation to take responsibility for the design. Historically, there have been conflicts in this role as the lead designer throughout the design process has strived to develop and safeguard the design quality. When the contractor employs the lead designer, the lead designer is contractually bound to follow the directions of the contractor, which may include accepting instruction that, in the lead designer's opinion,

Project lead roles (*continued*)

could compromise the design – it is therefore difficult for the lead designer to bring this issue to the attention of the client under the terms of their contract with the contractor. However, many quality contractors are now encouraging open conversations between their appointed designers and the client team in a quest to demonstrate an open approach to quality and differentiate them from what has become the established norm in design and build contracts.

Under the various roles described above, the activities of the project lead (with the possible exception of the design quality monitor) are broadly similar and involve the management and organisation of the following activities:

l arrange regular site meetings to monitor the progress of both the detailed design information and the construction works
l generally monitor the performance of the contractor
l monitor construction cash flow
l ensure that design information is being provided by the design team in accordance with the information release schedule (IRS)
l arrange site inspections by the design team
l monitor and obtain statutory approvals and inspections
l report to the client on progress
l ensure that procedures for payments are being followed
l implement Change Control Procedures
l identify and obtain any required works permits
l review and approve contractor's method statements to ensure that they provide a safe method of working
l anticipate and resolve issues on site
l monitor the response and resolution of technical queries (TQs) and requests for information (RFIs) and liaise with the design team on any unresolved aspects of the design
l quality-inspect the work to ensure that the required levels of workmanship are achieved.

Construction Programme

Programming, or time management, is one of the key functions of managing a project from a project lead's perspective. Failure to achieve established milestone dates will inevitably affect project costs. The project lead will have provided a Project Programme earlier in the process; this will generally cover all activities from inception to final handover. The durations and milestones within the Project Programme will have been determined by the project lead in collaboration with the design team and the client. The construction activities outlined in the Project Programme will therefore be indicative until validated by the contractor in the Construction Programme. This will be far more detailed in terms of content and will have incorporated timescales provided by the contractor's supply chain.

There are generally four steps in the creation of a successful Construction Programme:

Programme principles

1. **Planning:** establishing the anticipated activities, their logical sequence, constraints, interfaces and dependencies.
2. **Scheduling:** adding the durations and required resources and adjusting to relate to the site-specific constraints.
3. **Monitoring:** evaluating the subcontractor's progress against programme.
4. **Control:** exercising corrective action over unacceptable variances.

As part of the tender requirements, the contractor will have been required to submit a Construction Programme outlining all procurement, approval, mobilisation, manufacture, delivery and build periods anticipated during the construction process. The detail on the programme should clearly demonstrate all time periods that could impact the issue of the remaining detailed design information to be supplied by the designers. This will have been coordinated with the Stage 4 Design Programme to ensure that all designers understand the timescales for information release. The project lead should ensure proper interrogation of the Construction Programme

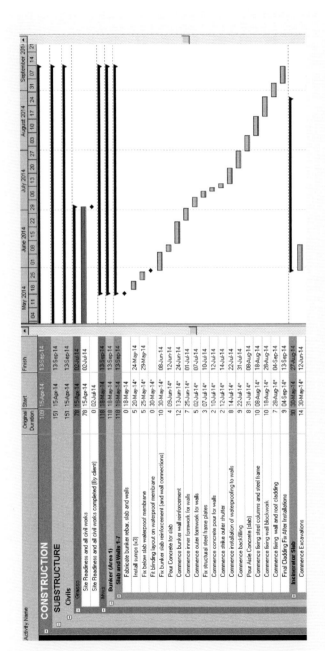

Figure 5.1   Example of a Gantt chart (Construction Programme)

by all disciplines of the core design team, as it will inform the sequence and time available for the remaining design work.

The Construction Programme would not normally be bound into the contract documentation as it will inevitably identify a series of interim milestones and deadlines that, if missed, provide the contractor with the means to claim delays against the design team.

Bar charts (Gantt charts, see figure 5.1) are the easiest way to describe sequence and activities in construction. A bar chart is formed with a list of activities, specifying the start date, duration of the activity and completion date of each activity, and then plotted into the project timescale. The level of detail of the bar chart will depend on the complexity of the project and the objectives that the schedule needs to communicate.

For projects that require a greater level of control and understanding of the activities and their dependencies, contractors will use a logic-linked bar chart. In this style of programme, each activity is linked to previous and subsequent activities, specifying that every activity has at least another one that must be completed prior to commencement of the subsequent activity. This is sometimes called the critical path method, and involves establishing specific dates and activities and assigning them with an early date, the first ideal date on which an activity can start, a late-start option, followed by finally specifying the last possible date by which this activity must be started to avoid delays in the overall construction process.

Offsite construction ·

An increasingly common technique for obtaining enhanced quality during the construction process is to utilise offsite construction technologies. There are several advantages to these:

I reduced onsite building time – offsite construction can be up to 50% faster than traditional build
I consequent reduction in risks to the Construction Programme
I reduced waste and fewer vehicle movements resulting in reduced noise and pollution
I costs will have been agreed at the outset, therefore greater cost certainty can be achieved
I improved health and safety.

Although there are significant programme benefits to be had during Construction, decisions will need to be made earlier in the design process (sometimes during Stage 3 on longer lead components) to provide technical details in sufficient time to allow the procurement and manufacture to take place prior to installation on site. This will require a greater level of coordination at the procurement stage to ensure that the offsite packages interface correctly both with each other and with the traditional elements of the build. If any of these interfaces are not properly resolved at the earlier stage, then the consequences can be more serious than with traditional construction techniques as correcting the components manufactured offsite can prove problematic outside of the factory environment.

Health and Safety Strategy during Construction

Prior to a contractor's start on site, the project lead will need to establish that the contractor's systems and processes are properly established before work commences. During Construction, successful health and safety management relies on clear and effective communication. As a result the project lead should seek to make health and safety the first item on any meeting agenda and actively promote/support the contractor and regularly assess how and what they are doing with regard to staff, visitors and the public. Other initiatives requiring consideration might include an open policy of rewarding or reprimanding personnel in order to educate on incident reporting, use of mandatory permits to control activities, consistent use of visual communication to support verbal communication, and encouraging staff, visitors and contractors to proactively contribute to safety management.

Detailed below is just some of the guidance on the design team's responsibilities regarding health and safety during a construction project.

Design team responsibilities regarding health and safety

Everyone
- Understand the client's health and safety expectations
- Comply with personal protective equipment (PPE) requirements
- Cooperate with others and coordinate measures
- Report any risks

Design team responsibilities regarding health and safety (*continued*)

- Take account of and apply the general principles of prevention when carrying out duties
- Provide necessary information or implement practices to comply/meet with health and safety performance drivers
- Consider health and safety of the public

The client

- Understand that there is a cost attributed to the safe delivery of a project
- Establish health and safety performance goals and set these in the context of other project success drivers
- Set targets for improvement, monitor and record achievements
- Check competence and resources of all appointed contractors
- Ensure that there are suitable management arrangements for the project, including welfare facilities
- Allow sufficient time and resources for all stages
- Provide pre-construction information to designers and the contractor

Design team and other external consultants

- In conjunction with the project lead, undertake a health and safety awareness workshop
- Consider temporary and permanent conditions of the construction activities
- Consider health and safety during construction as well as during the day-to-day use of the building, including maintenance
- Consider the use of offsite prefabrication and manufacture
- Eliminate hazards and reduce risks during design
- Engage the appropriate specialist contractors' input in contributing towards safe design
- Provide information about remaining risks
- Arrange periodic health and safety review meetings and see that corrective actions are allocated to those responsible and monitor implementation
- Collect health and safety information from the contractor

Contractor

- Prepare and maintain the health and safety plan, ensuring that any amendments are promptly communicated
- Establish health and safety performance systems to comply with requirements of key performance drivers
- Prepare, as appropriate, Risk Assessments and method statements and communicate them to the proper parties

Design team responsibilities regarding health and safety (*continued*)

- Plan, manage and monitor own work and that of workers, including reasonable directions and site rules
- Ensure that PPE is used by and available to all
- Undertake regular health and safety inspections and audits
- Check competence of appointees and obtain key health and safety information from them to update the health and safety plan
- Ensure that all workers have site inductions and any further information and training needed for the work
- Ensure that site safety procedures are clear and applied to all
- Ensure that there are adequate welfare facilities for workers
- Liaise with the consultants regarding ongoing design and elimination of risks
- Inform the project lead of reportable accidents, diseases and dangerous occurrences
- Prepare and submit the health and safety file to the client incorporating 'As-constructed' Information and operation and maintenance manuals.

PPE – personal protective equipment is equipment or clothing required to be worn under current health and safety legislation. This includes, among other things: Hi-Vis outer garments, steel toe-capped boots, protective glasses and gloves.

HSE guidance

For further reading on health and safety in construction, please visit the Health and Safety Executive's website at www.hse.gov.uk/

Handover Strategy

The Handover Strategy is a reference document that is to be used by all members of the design team in understanding their role in achieving a satisfactory handover of any project. It should be concise and easy to use and therefore will be made up largely of clearly presented schedules and checklists. The client will usually be taking handover of an unfamiliar environment and it is in the project lead's interest that the client is acquainted with the building through inductions and manuals received prior to occupation.

The Handover Strategy should include the following main elements:

- Schedule of roles and responsibilities for the project team
- Criteria for completion and criteria for handover, including all activities necessary to achieve a quality handover
- Completion and handover programme, showing timescales and interdependencies
- Training schedule.

In addition to this, the Handover Strategy should include a number of more detailed checklists, such as:

I completion checklist – identifies all activities, paperwork and approval items that are prerequisites for accepting the project as complete and the for client accepting it at handover, and identifies who is responsible for providing and/or compiling each item

I commissioning checklist – gives a comprehensive list of all aspects of services that need to be demonstrated, witnessed and commissioned and identifies who is involved in each of the activities; it is advisable that the consulting engineer creates and manages this document

I spares checklist – gives a comprehensive list of all the items that the contractor is required or can be expected to provide to the client on handover, including training; it may be appropriate for the contractor to compile this list but the project lead should, as a minimum, check the contract documents for spares requirements.

During the earlier design stages, the details of how the works should be commissioned and handed over within the live environment need to be considered.

With a specific view to handover and commissioning, the project lead must ensure that the Handover and Close Out procedures and expectations are properly detailed within the tender documentation and that all the constraints on the building services installation due to live environments are clearly stated. This should include a detailed phasing programme, information on how snags would be controlled throughout the project, testing and commissioning expectations with regard to witnessing and client training requirements.

This will provide a level of reassurance to the design team and the client that the contractor fully understands the process required to achieve Practical Completion and has priced accordingly. Furthermore, it must be a prerequisite of the tender response that the contractor details their approach and methodology using leading-edge techniques, such as electronic snag management systems.

Prior to contract award, the contractor's quality plan should be properly reviewed to check that there is sufficient provision for appropriate and proactive snag clearance systems. This will enable the contractor to manage their own snags and defects process effectively and progressively but with transparency to the client and the design team as it occurs. Given the appropriate time and training, such systems provide a standard and structured approach, with all consultants integrating into the process so that the client or their facilities team can clearly see the standard of quality that is being achieved.

During the construction period on larger, more complex projects, it is worth appointing a construction and building services clerk of works and a commissioning specialist in addition to the core design team disciplines. While it is the contractor's responsibility to complete the works in accordance with the contract documents, it is very valuable to bring in specialists who can work on behalf of the client but with the contractor to ensure that systems are tested, commissioned and handed over in accordance with the contract. These teams are all expected to provide a report and list of defects that exist at Practical Completion as well as remaining with the project under direction of the project lead supporting the client or their facilities team until close out of any subsequent issues during occupation.

The completion strategy will also include a list of pro forma required. This list will provide a checklist for the project lead in preparing the necessary documentation for use at completion and handover. The list will include all documents that need to be prepared and will also identify who is responsible for producing them.

Finally, the completion strategy will include explanatory text setting out how various aspects of the completion and handover activities will be managed, for example:

I   demonstrations, witnessing and commissioning; snagging, inspections and sign-off
I   issue of certificates and notices
I   defects management.

In addition to the above, the project lead should ensure that the contractor sets up a series of training workshops with the client and their facilities management team, preferably video-recorded so that the facilities management team can refer back to the session. The contractor should also provide a summary schedule of the systems that have been installed and the regular maintenance requirements as a user-friendly 'quick reference' guide.

Continuous collation of operating and maintenance (O&M) manuals

A regular stumbling block on projects is the timely completion of O&M manuals. It will be necessary to track the production of the O&M manuals from early in the construction period to ensure that they are being produced in line with the client's requirements. This is an effective strategy that will contribute to them being available punctually at handover.

Defining what Practical Completion actually means is essential in making sure there are no misinterpretations on the part of any participants in the project, including the client. One approach to handover is to instigate a 'countdown to completion' process. It is advisable to hold regular sessions with the client, contractor, facilities team and relevant members of the design team from several weeks before Practical Completion.

This procedure will maintain focus on commissioning programmes, training schedules, O&M manual compilation and witnessing regimes and will allow the project lead to actively track progress before it is too late. These documents should be reviewed regularly to ensure that, as handover approaches, all parties are aware of their actions and responsibilities. The result should be that, at handover, there are no surprises for the project team.

Soft Landings

The Soft Landings initiative, developed by BSRIA, recognises and overcomes problems beyond building completion and handover and should be included in the Handover Strategy. The Soft Landings approach means that designers and contractors remain involved with buildings and their users after completion. The advice will help the client during the first period of operation, in calibrating the systems, and ensuring that they understand how to manage and make the most of their new building.

Soft Landings

For further reading on BSRIA Soft Landings please visit BSRIA's website at www.bsria.co.uk/services/design/soft-landings/

The Soft Landings recommendations increase the duties of the design team during handover and for the first three years of occupation, following the process outlined below:

Soft Landings process

Step 1: Inception and briefing
This provides more time for constructive dialogue between the project lead, the design team, the contractor and the client.

Step 2: Design development and review
This will bring the design team together to review issues from precedent projects and examine how the building will work from the point of view of the systems manager or individual user.

Step 3: Pre-handover
This allows building users to spend more time understanding interfaces and systems prior to occupation.

Soft Landings process (*continued*)

Step 4: Initial aftercare
This provides continuing involvement by the client and the design and building team, benefiting from lessons learned and occupant satisfaction surveys.

Step 5: Years 1–3 extended aftercare and Post-occupancy Evaluation
Completing the development cycle for future projects, this stage closes the loop between design expectation and reality.

Defining Practical Completion

It is useful for the project lead to properly define the term 'Practical Completion' prior to the close-out activities to ensure that a collectively agreed interpretation is in place throughout the design team and, more importantly, that the contractor is in agreement. When the contractor informs the project lead that the works are complete, the project lead will organise a session with the contractor to confirm that the construction has been completed to the standard stipulated in the contract documents.

Practical Completion

If the project lead and client are confident that the building can be received in a partially incomplete state, the certificate of Practical Completion should incorporate a clause confirming that the contractor commits to rectifying specific items within an agreed timescale. These items must be catalogued and appended to the certificate and the copy of the schedule passed to the project lead and occupiers.

The handover checklists should be completed by the design team and handed to the project lead for the record.

Partial possession

When, with the cooperation of the contractor, the client wishes to take possession of certain areas of the works, the process for receiving the works must be applied to each part to be occupied as though it were itself a complete building. Retention money will be released pro rata according to the value of the section in terms of the whole works and the defects liability period will be applicable to each section as it is handed over to the client.

It is important to outline the difference between partial possession and sectional completion. Partial possession is an event that was not envisaged or allowed for when the Building Contract was signed. Sectional completion is an activity that was allowed for by the inclusion of a sectional completion clause in the contract.

Sectional completion

When the Building Contract has been specifically amended for completion in sections by the inclusion of the sectional completion clause, an obligation is imposed on the contractor to complete the project in stages with specific reference to the requirements included within the contract. Certificates of sectional completion and certificates of making good defects will be necessary for each portion of the works.

Zero defects

A project's success is dependent upon the whole project team having a common goal and the commitment to achieve this goal together. A 'zero defects' approach is the aspiration to reach the end of the construction stage of a project with all defects identified and rectified as the work progresses. This means that the effort required at completion is minimised, as there should be no defects to rectify immediately prior to handover. Construction requires the involvement of many people whose input is made at various stages throughout the duration of the project, including the design stages. The interfaces are so numerous that to achieve zero defects requires a team that shares a common goal and works together. The project lead will need to provide the constant, unifying force throughout the project, combining the outputs of each of these parties to produce the final coordinated product. Great emphasis should therefore be placed on teamwork and collaborative working, learning from each other and accepting the challenges of each project within a structured environment.

Achievement of zero defects at completion is a challenging but achievable target. The degree of planning and commitment by all parties necessary to meet such a challenge should not be underestimated.

In order to achieve the best possible quality at handover, the project lead will have to adopt a process as follows:

I Prepare a stage plan of work covering the completion phase of the project, identifying the objective (ie completion on time with zero defects), the process by which the objective will be delivered and the necessary output (including the issue of relevant certificates and records).

I Integrate the stage plan of work with the contractor's completion programme and verify that the programme is achievable.

I Ensure that the programme includes full and adequate provision for testing, commissioning, witnessing of tests, inspections and all completion activities.

I Adopt a progressive approvals process, identifying milestones for completion of sections of the project so that inspections can take place at the earliest possible stage.

I Establish quality criteria through the Employer's Requirements and agreed quality benchmarking samples of completed work early in the construction process.

I Expand on the definition of Practical Completion in the building contract to establish a definitive statement of quality required to enable completion to be certified.

I Establish a rigorous process of inspections and follow-up inspections, demonstrating attention to detail and an intention to achieve best quality.

It is also important to 'snag the building' informally with the design team as it is completed per element; this process should then be formally recorded as observations to the contractor and the contractor's progress

Achieving zero defects

Periodic inspections during the construction period that establish quality benchmarks for all areas of the building as they are constructed will help to align the expectations of the client and the contractor. Making sure that the detailed specifications, alongside other objectives contained within the Employer's Requirements, provide the project lead with very clear standards of workmanship, acceptable construction tolerances and sample texture/colour ranges. This then becomes the yardstick by which quality demands can be placed on the contractor.

on actions resulting from those observations should be reviewed monthly. This will ensure that the contractor is actively engaged with the team and monitoring the achieved quality levels as the building is completed and prior to completion, thereby ensuring that any defects and any snagging at completion are minimised.

'As-constructed' Information

'As-constructed' Information illustrates the final installed project configuration (whether physical or functional). It indicates any construction deviations and shows all features of the project. These drawings provide a permanent record of 'as-built' conditions and function as key references for future maintenance processes.

'As-constructed' Information

'As-constructed' Information can include any or all of the following:

- architectural layouts, plans, sections and elevations
- architectural details
- structural layouts
- structural details
- mechanical services
- electrical services
- highway layouts
- drainage and water supply
- architectural specifications
- mechanical specifications.

In addition to the drawings, which give the final details, there is also a need to provide specific details of the materials used in the construction of the project. These must be contained within the O&M manuals, of which the drawings form an integral element.

It is recommended that the 'As-constructed' Information is reviewed regularly for accuracy and completeness by the contractor as part of the monthly payment process. 'As-constructed' Information is not simply a requirement at the end of a project but must be available on the project site at all times. The following checklist provides some advice on content and presentation:

I   Vague phrases such as 'equal to' and 'similar to' should be crossed out and replaced with the specific information used during the construction process.

I   The exact details of changes or additional information must be provided.

I   All necessary information of contractor's designed systems must be included.

I   All unexpected obstructions found on site must be recorded.

I   Changes made due to the final inspection process must be detailed.

I   If possible, 'as-built' drawings should highlight deleted items, added items and special information or details.

I   Specific actions should be referred to rather than referencing change order numbers or related documents.

I   Changes must be described in writing.

I   Revision notes and corrections should be added to all affected views, general notes, specific notes, profiles and schedules.

I   All related shop drawings must be added to the 'As-constructed' Information set.

I   The index sheet must be updated to show the latest drawing changes or additions.

I   References to underground utilities must be specific, showing exact location, depth and material used.

I   When finished, the title sheet must be stamped with 'RECORD DRAWING AS-BUILT' including the contractor's name, the date and other relevant information.

I   Finally, a searchable CD containing the 'As-constructed' Information must be prepared.

Chapter summary   5

The construction period in any project is the culmination of all the hard work by a myriad of participants during the briefing and design of the project. It should be the most enjoyable and straightforward period of a building's inception for all of those involved as, theoretically, the process involves following a clear set of directions to a set time and within an agreed budget. This may seem slightly idealistic and the reality can be somewhat different as relationships become stretched due to misinterpretations, conflicting opinions and poor workmanship. One of the keys to a successful construction phase lies in the completeness and accuracy of the information used as the basis of the Building Contract.

This would suggest that traditional procurement strategies will always result in a less confrontational experience during construction; however, there are still many challenges that may arise on site that may not have been envisaged during the earlier design stages. These cover the whole spectrum of human nature, which is notoriously difficult to legislate against, and factors such as change, indecision, bias, incompetency, obstruction and deceit will all contribute to challenge what should remain a truly collaborative process.

The solution must therefore lie in a genuinely open and trusting approach by all parties; an environment where everyone pursues the same goals and understands from the start that a problem for one party is a problem for all. The project lead's approach is the key to unlocking this goal and they must ensure that their behaviour generates and encourages this culture of cooperation.

The smooth handover of any project will be dependent on early consideration of the client's ability to take over the building and operate and maintain the complex systems commissioned at completion. These considerations should be comprehensively outlined within the Handover Strategy.

The Soft Landings initiative embedded within the Handover Strategy begins at the start of any project and is not only relevant to the activities at handover. It promotes better briefing, demonstrable performance benchmarking, sense-checking of the design principles and procurement strategies, a progressive Handover Strategy and extended involvement of the design team, providing an extra level of aftercare.

Handover and Close Out

Chapter overview

During Stage 6 the project team's priorities will be to facilitate the successful handover of the building in line with the Project Programme and, in the period immediately following, conclude all aspects of the Building Contract, including the inspection of defects as they are rectified or the production of certification required by the Building Contract.

The key coverage in this chapter is as follows:

Core Objectives

Roles during completion and handover

Commissioning

Setting up Post-occupancy Evaluations

Defects liability period

Introduction

Towards the end of the construction period, the project lead will need to set up a series of countdown meetings to ensure that the close out activities can be identified and prioritised with the contractor, the design team and the client to ensure a smooth and effective handover of the building. The project lead will then monitor all actions at this stage as part of the overall Handover Strategy.

Participation and dialogue with the client and the stakeholders is to be encouraged, and they should be invited to visit the site regularly to express their views on the construction works as they approach completion. They will also need to be physically aware of what they are receiving well in advance so that any concerns or issues can be openly discussed and addressed before they occupy the building.

The project lead should be actively engaged with the client and the design team in monitoring the achieved quality levels throughout the entirety of the works to ensure that any defects and any snagging at completion is always minimised.

Prior to handover, the building will need to be snagged (checked for unacceptable workmanship) with the design team and the contractor. Any defects during the earlier section of the works will be communicated formally to the contractor as quality benchmarks and progress against the benchmarks reviewed monthly. A more rigorous process of quality inspections occurs closer to completion to provide formal records of defects that can be checked off as they are completed in accordance with the contract documentation.

The project lead will have to ensure that the contractor sets up a series of training workshops with the client and their facilities management team. The contractor should also provide a schedule of the systems that have been installed and the regular maintenance requirements as a user-friendly 'quick reference' guide so that the client can occupy and start to enjoy their new facility at day one – handover.

What are the Core Objectives of this stage?

The Core Objectives of the RIBA Plan of Work 2013 at Stage 6 are:

	6 Handover and Close Out
Tasks ▼	
Core Objectives	Handover of building and conclusion of **Building Contract**.

The design team's scope of services during this stage will be dictated by professional services agreements, which should be aligned with the procurement strategy and Handover Strategy. Tasks carried out as part of the established Handover Strategy might include the inspection of defects as they are rectified or the production of certification of completion in relation to the Building Contract.

Tasks in relation to the Handover Strategy can be wide-ranging, and may include:

I attending Feedback workshops
I considering how any lessons learned might be applied on future projects
I preparing for the initial Post-occupancy Evaluation that considers whether the desired Project Outcomes have been achieved
I undertaking tasks in relation to commissioning or ensuring the successful completion, operation and management of the building.

Roles during completion and handover

Each organisation involved with a project will have a Schedule of Services as defined within their professional services agreements. However, it is important that the roles and responsibilities of each organisation are agreed with and communicated across the whole design team. A set of typical roles and responsibilities that may be adopted during the completion phase of the project is set out below:

Typical roles at completion

Project lead
- Monitoring progress
- Ensuring that regular site inspection is carried out by the project team

Contract administrator (dependent on contract form)
- Issuing contract variations
- Issuing taking-over certificates

Lead designer/architect
- Arranging planning authority/building control completion as necessary
- Site inspections
- Snagging and defects inspections
- Leading the design team/design coordination

Structural engineer
- Site inspections
- Snagging and defects inspections
- Reporting to lead designer/engineer as appropriate

M&E services/sustainability engineer
- Site inspections
- Snagging and defects inspections
- Reporting to lead designer/engineer as appropriate

Cost manager
- Cost monitoring
- Cost reporting
- Valuation of contractor's work

Closing out the Building Contract

About two weeks before the date when Practical Completion of the project is due, the project lead (or the contract administrator) will need to arrange a handover meeting on site with the contractor. Where a building services consultant has been involved in the design they should also be in attendance. Any minor defect modifications that the contractor is required to carry out prior to Practical Completion can be agreed and implemented.

Once the identified defects have been completed, the client/occupier should be invited to walk around the building and the project lead/ contract administrator should be in a position to confirm the anticipated date for Practical Completion with the contractor, identifying any minor outstanding items of work and a timetable to rectify them.

Under the terms of most Building Contracts, the contract administrator will be required to issue to the contractor a certificate of Practical Completion in some form; this states that the works have been completed in accordance with the Building Contract. To enable the contract administrator to issue this certificate, they will require confirmation letters from the key members of the design team, stating that, in their opinion, the works are complete and that the certificate of Practical Completion can be issued. At the same time as issuing the certificate of Practical Completion, the contract administrator will also be required to issue a full list of outstanding items or defects, which will not substantially affect the beneficial use of the works.

At the point of issuing the certificate of Practical completion, it is the responsibility of the client to arrange insurance cover for the building as the contractor's insurances will be ceased.

Managing the client's expectations at handover

For many clients, the only time they realise what they are actually getting is when they physically witness the construction of the design proposals on site. This can be a challenge for the project lead at this late stage as, despite constant reviews and sign-offs throughout the design stages, the client will inevitably see

Managing the client's expectations at handover
(**continued**)

something they did not expect. Records of all decisions made will usually demonstrate that everything has been done with the full buy-in of the client so the temptation at this stage to make alterations to work on site as the contractor approaches completion should be avoided – it will confuse the process, add cost, result in late handover of the works and affect quality at a time when the contractor is focusing on completion activities.

Commissioning

The process of commissioning needs to be identified at an early stage in the project and involving the necessary consultants at that stage is essential to ensure the benefits of commissioning are genuinely delivered.

It is important for the project lead to safeguard the time required for commissioning so that it is not compressed or carried out on incomplete systems. In order to achieve optimum performance from the building services, the project lead must ensure that a planned and detailed Project Programme identifies the key activities from specification, through construction and commissioning, and into the post-occupancy stage.

A key role at this stage is the appointment by the client of an independent commissioning engineer, to manage and coordinate the commissioning in collaboration with the contractor. The scope of the commissioning engineer should be identified in the contract at the outset. At the commencement of the project, a commissioning strategy needs to be prepared and incorporated into the Building Contract that will form an essential part of the handover process. The input of this specialist is vital in ensuring that the system design is properly commissioned. As discussed in the previous chapter, a framework called 'Soft Landings' has been instigated by BSRIA; this has been created to improve the handing over of a building. This framework is a process that helps to smooth the transition from handover to occupancy. In the early stages of commissioning, Risk Assessments, method statements and system trackers must be prepared and these must be monitored throughout the process.

The process of commissioning involves the instigation of a systematic quality assurance process, which is intended to reassure the client that the building systems have been installed and are functioning correctly.

Once the commissioning process has been implemented, the commissioning engineer will produce a systems manual. The systems manual is important – becoming an operating manual for the client. However, the creation of this manual is not the extent of the commissioning engineer's responsibility – they must also produce verification checklists and functional test schedules and complete seasonal or deferred systems testing. The commissioning engineer may also participate in training the building's users to make sure that they are competent to run and operate the building's systems efficiently, in order to achieve the performance levels for which the systems are designed.

Handover of small projects

On smaller, less complicated projects, the handover procedures may consist of a straightforward demonstration of the functions of a system, an explanation of the optimal settings for controls and the issuing of manufacturer's instructions.

However, on larger, more complex projects it is not unusual for the handover activities to have their own budget and programmes, in order to ensure that all elements of project handover are properly planned and executed in a professional and expedient manner.

Defects liability period (DLP)

Under most Building Contracts, one of the contractor's main obligations is to execute and complete the works to the quality and workmanship standards set out in the contract. The DLP is intended to ensure that the client has recourse to require the contractor to return to the building to rectify defective work which becomes apparent during a predetermined period contained within the Building Contract. In effect, the defects liability provision recognises that defects will appear after completion and includes the requirement to rectify those defects to ensure the works are completed to the required standards in line with the Building Contract.

Ensuring that the contractor is responsible for the repairs is usually less expensive and more efficient than appointing another contractor to do the work.

Immediately after the contract administrator has issued the certificate of Practical Completion and the building has entered the DLP, the contract administrator must arrange with the project lead a meeting with the client and the contractor on site, including relevant members of the design team. At this meeting the building will be officially handed over to the client, with the operating and maintenance (O&M) manuals, and the operation of all plant should be demonstrated.

At this meeting, the project lead should also agree with the client that, during the DLP, all defects, breakages or failures will be reported directly to the project lead and no instructions be given to the contractor's personnel, who may subsequently visit the site.

The project lead must decide which items are defects in accordance with the contract and which, if any, are general wear and tear items. In the case of wear and tear, the project lead may ask the contract administrator to issue an instruction to the contractor to correct the works.

During the DLP the project lead will have to agree the timescales for any repair works with the contractor and the client.

In most contracts, the client will usually retain a portion of the contract sum as insurance to make sure the contractor meets their obligations during the DLP. This is called 'retention' and is generally 5% of the amount certified as due to the contractor on an interim certificate.

Chapter summary 6

Stage 6 Handover and Close Out now provides the client with the necessary support from the design team to occupy the building confident that any defects will have been identified, monitored and closed out. The systems and controls within the building services will also have had any teething problems ironed out with input from the original designer rather than the client's facilities management staff, who are likely to lack familiarity with the specification of the installation.

Post-occupancy Evaluations will now become the norm and will allow clients and design teams alike to benefit from lessons learned with a more formal measurement of the success of both the building and the process.

The DLP provides a mechanism by which defects not evident at completion can be rectified by the contractor over the pre-agreed period included within the Building Contract.

Stage 7

In Use

Chapter overview

Stage 7 In Use is an important new addition to the Plan of Work 2013 and is intended to benefit from the Post-occupancy Evaluations, Feedback and lessons learned to both the client and the design team. Potential residence by members of the design team in the new building during Stage 6 will have provided reassurance that the process is complete, with the design team helping to overcome teething problems and providing proper guidance and explanation of the often complex systems installed within the building.

The key coverage in this chapter is as follows:

Core Objectives

Post-occupancy Evaluation

Feedback

Key performance indicators

Performance monitoring

Updates to Project Information

Computer-aided facilities management

Project Objectives

Project team

Professional services agreement

Programme and budget

Client interaction

Introduction

This stage consists of reviewing the scheme in use by means of many different methods, from responding to the Post-occupancy Evaluation/questionnaires and performance monitoring through to consultants taking up residence in the completed scheme during the early part of occupation. The addition of this stage also provides room for further developments to benefit from lessons learned and the knowledge obtained by consultants and the client alike.

Being a new addition to the RIBA Plan of Work, this stage is likely to evolve as design teams and clients encounter and understand the most beneficial interaction techniques. This will develop further depending on the type of scheme that is reviewed during the In Use stage of its life cycle.

What are the Core Objectives of this stage?

The Core Objectives of the RIBA Plan of Work 2013 at Stage 7 are:

Tasks ▼	**7** **In Use**
Core Objectives	Undertake **In Use** services in accordance with **Schedule of Services**.

At present, it is rare for a project team commissioned at Stage 1 to continue to provide professional services beyond Stage 6. The exception would be the Handover Strategy services that occur in years 1 to 3 post occupancy, when such services currently end. The Core Objective of this stage is fully dependent on the Schedule of Services agreed with the client. Understanding the information or services that are required by the client and the level of interaction expected by the design team is key from the outset of the stage. Having understood what the stage outputs are, the project lead should focus on strategic thinking around the project team inputs for the stage, the programme and the actual outputs to be produced. These could include comparative studies of actual systems performance versus original design criteria, response to staff productivity assessments or staff satisfaction questionnaires.

Completion of Stage 7 will not be part of the main design team professional services agreements and therefore will require new agreements or extensions to the original professional services agreements. If new appointments are required for the completion of the stage, clear definition of the Schedule of Services is essential from the commencement of the stage to fully understand the participation required and to coordinate the inputs of the project team in accordance with the client objectives for the stage. It should also be noted that the undertaking of Stage 7 may not be by the incumbent design team but could be carried out by an independent body separately appointed or from within the client's own team depending on their level of familiarity with the project or extent of industry knowledge.

Client objectives may differ depending on the facility and thus will need to be reflected in the scope of the design team input required. Different evaluation techniques, discussed in the sections below, require varying levels of expertise and input and therefore may require alternative discipline involvement.

Early commitment to Stage 7 appointments

It is preferable for the client to commit to undertaking Stage 7 during the commencement of the project at Stages 0 and 1. This would ensure that the strategic and briefing documentation outlines the key performance indicators (KPIs) for the project, which would be reflected in the evaluation of its performance in use to provide a meaningful review. Such reviews drive the construction industry forward in understanding elements that are successful and others that may need to be executed differently in future phases or projects. Such knowledge can therefore inform and improve earlier stages for future projects.

Post-occupancy Evaluation

The Post-occupancy Evaluation can be split into two areas: reviewing the success of the initial delivery and assessing the performance of the scheme once in use.

The process of collating data can be achieved through the use of questionnaires and/or interviews. Such information gathering can be employed among the end users and client team to gain an understanding of how the scheme is performing by those for whom it was designed.

Typical Post-occupancy Evaluation contents

1.0 Introduction and questionnaire objectives
2.0 Participant information
   2.1 Relation to scheme
   2.2 How often used
   2.3 When used
   2.4 What used for
3.0 Impressions of the scheme
   3.1 Does it meet your requirements?
   3.2 Top five positives of the scheme?
   3.3 Top five negatives of the scheme?
   3.4 Any improvements to be considered?
   3.5 Any elements to be changed or added?
4.0 Would you recommend this scheme to others?
5.0 Frequency of use
   5.1 Will you revisit the scheme?
6.0 Quality perceptions
7.0 Engagement with the community
   7.1 Did you feel engaged throughout the process?
8.0 Further comments
9.0 Contact information if available

The questions that form part of this exercise should be project specific and may also be influenced by the project's own KPIs, discussed in a following section.

Feedback

Feedback and lessons learned ideally should be undertaken by the design team following completion even if Stage 7 is not commissioned by the client. Feedback should be received from a number of different sources, such as the client, end users and other stakeholders, for example local communities. Distribution among diverse user groups would provide a more thorough review and would help the design team to understand how successfully the different parties interacted with the scheme. Feedback can be carried out through such methods as questionnaires and interviews.

Elements that can be reviewed as part of the Feedback stage could be:

| the scheme's performance against established KPIs

- the performance of the scheme against the design criteria and specifications
- communication of the project team
- interaction between the client team and the design team
- quality of information produced
- accuracy of the operating and maintenance (O&M) manuals.

Concerns/issues will be logged, categorised and reviewed at the end of the pre-agreed periods to identify which still pose any problems. It is common for most of the original issues to have dropped away as people adjust to their new environment and so items left on the list become genuine issues that can then be addressed.

Bedding-in periods

The project lead should encourage the client to allow their building to 'bed in' for an agreed period of time before any end user-led changes are implemented. This approach allows end users to acclimatise to the building and the facilities management team to understand new systems before any 'tweaks' are made.

An online questionnaire is a useful tool to capture the views of the end users on the building's performance and should be separated into different categories for easy assessment. An online questionnaire system is quick and efficient; ensuring that a greater level of returns from staff is achieved.

The data can be presented in many ways, but the diagrams in figure 7.1 demonstrate in graphic form how opinions formed about the new building compared to the opinions of the users when asked the same questions of their existing premises (pre and post).

These opinions can then be reviewed with the client and the design team to then develop and implement a corrective plan that will help clients to optimise their facility's potential post completion.

Post-occupancy Evaluations

For further reading on Post-occupancy Evaluations please visit the BRE website at www.bre.co.uk

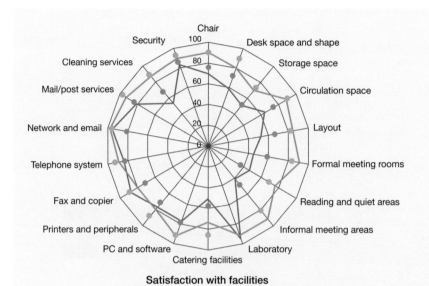

Satisfaction with facilities

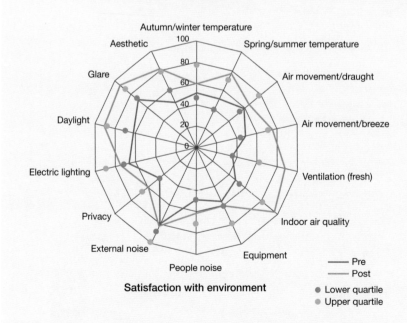

Satisfaction with environment

Figure 7.1   Communicating the Post-occupancy Evaluation results

Lessons learned should also be drawn via Feedback from within the design team. Elements that worked and parts of the process that did not work so well should be reviewed and understood for future projects.

O&M manuals detail the day-to-day procedures required for the safe and efficient operation and maintenance of the building's systems, as well as references to applicable codes and standards. The manuals are also useful for training and employee orientation.

Key performance indicators

The KPIs for the scheme would ideally have been established at the project outset to enable beneficial reviews to take place through review of the benchmarked indicators. Reviewing the performance of the scheme against its original KPIs requires objectivity from the body undertaking the exercise.

Depending on the KPI to be assessed, different evaluation methods may be used including end user surveys, testing of the building's environmental performance levels and surveys of how particular areas are used. The importance of establishing KPIs can be demonstrated during this stage and determines the relevance of information secured for future projects.

Further areas that can be reviewed are:

I Interactions in the space; do the floor layouts work?
I Aesthetic qualities
I Comfort and ease of use
I Does the running cost of the scheme match the original client aspirations and design criteria?
I Does the project meet the KPIs?
I Does the project meet the originally defined sustainability targets?

Performance monitoring

Performance monitoring can be undertaken in a number of different ways depending on the element of the scheme requiring assessment. Aspects such as the effectiveness of internal climate control, natural ventilation or the overall suitability of the building management systems (BMS) can be easily measured through continuous tests throughout the first years of operation. This can be reviewed at different times of the day to reflect the level of use.

The timing of the review is important. Performance assessments should not be carried out during initial project use stages, while the systems are bedding in and still being adjusted to perform at the required levels. Allowing a sensible period of time to elapse will also ensure that the end users and maintenance teams have sufficient time to become acquainted with the scheme and interact with it in a more natural way than potentially they would in the initial set-up period.

Updates to Project Information

Depending on the Schedule of Services, the client team may require 'as-constructed' drawings and O&M manuals to be updated during the life of the scheme. This may be due to floor layouts being adapted during the early occupation of the building or new maintenance systems being installed. This may also be linked to other feedback methods being employed in the project, such as updates required due to underperformance of systems, feedback from residences or end user requirements not being met, either through misinterpretation or the discovery by the client of an emerging operational need that differs from the original brief.

It must be noted that refurbishments or floor plan upgrades may also be undertaken at this stage with the process recommencing from Stage 0 to properly plan for the future anticipated uses of the building.

Computer-aided facilities management (CAFM)

CAFM includes the preparation and implementation of IT-based systems in recently completed building projects. A typical CAFM system will be a combination of CAD and/or a referenced database with specific capabilities for use by client facilities management teams. The emergence of BIM technologies now makes this an extremely useful instrument in the management of new buildings post occupation. They are, however, only as good as the information uploaded during the design and specification process.

The advantages of a CAFM system are:

I   helping the facilities management team to ensure that the organisation's assets are fully optimised in a cost effective manner, while providing tangible benefits throughout the building's life span

I   supporting management of both the facility and operations; for example, the activities associated with managerial, practical and technical facilities management tasks during the building's operation

I   providing a platform for planning and execution of facilities management during the lifetime of the building.

CAFM systems can be made up from a selection of technologies and information sources and can also be linked back to the client's asset management systems. These could comprise a variety of database systems, CAD documentation, BIM information and links to other procedures, such as a computerised maintenance management system (CMMS). Most CAFM systems are now live databases accessed via the internet and offer many characteristics comprising scheduling and analysis capabilities. The information can be amassed from a multiplicity of sources through IT interfaces and data can be stored, recovered and analysed from a single data-store.

Project Objectives

The stage objectives must be defined at the outset to determine what needs to be reviewed and how the reviews will be carried out. The project lead must work with the client team to ensure that they understand the options available to them and which are likely to be the most beneficial and applicable to the scheme.

As the objectives for the stage should have been defined at the project outset, these will need to be reviewed to confirm that they are still applicable to the scheme following completion and occupation.

Project team

Depending on the Schedule of Services, the evaluation techniques to be adopted and even the project itself, the design team members required to take part in Stage 7 may vary. This will also be linked to the areas of focus within the KPIs, if defined at the beginning of the process.

Professional services agreement

As previously discussed, Stage 7 is unlikely to form part of the original project team professional services agreements. Addenda to the main agreements or new contracts may need to be agreed prior to the commencement of the stage. If aligned with the original professional services agreements or the Building Contract, KPIs may be extended to be assessed during Stage 7.

The project lead must ensure that the professional services agreements and the Building Contract to which all parties are committed defines the programme, scope and budget clearly, as discussed below.

Programme and budget

A new programme and budget for this stage will need to be produced and included in a new professional services agreement and must be carefully monitored to assess progress. It is important to define the objectives, adequately resource the team and identify who will be undertaking the various activities required. The length of the stage should also be defined as early as possible and should be limited to a particular scope as making sure that the client obtains the most accurate and useful data may prove to be a long-term exercise.

Client interaction

Once defined within the Schedule of Services, Building Contract and Project Programme, client interaction has to be carefully managed to ensure there is a clear understanding of what the design team needs to provide. Client expectations must also be fully understood in order to determine how they can best be delivered.

Client becoming dependent on consultant input

It is important to align client expectations with what the design team is tasked to deliver. Clients can become dependent on having consultant input during the In Use phase. Such dependence may become challenging to manage if it pushes the consultant team beyond their agreed scope and budget.

If the consultant team is also part of the project for a prolonged amount of time, the client may become dependent on having their input into the running and updates to the scheme. This may prove problematic to both client and end user once the consultant's scope is complete and they no longer interface with the project in this way.

Chapter summary 7

Stage 7 In Use, even though a new addition to the RIBA Plan of Work 2013, represents an important progression, taking schemes further to understand how they programme and learn for future developments. This can produce important data to improve the industry as a whole and incorporate a learning culture, which the industry has previously lacked due to the one–off nature of projects and short-term project teams.

The outputs of this stage can be in many forms depending on what is required: performance evaluations, lessons learned, performance monitoring and so on. Defining this stage properly can help to eliminate fee overspends and programme overruns and facilitate understanding on the part of the client regarding what they will see during the stage.

Project leadership glossary

BREEAM

The Building Research Establishment Environmental Assessment Methodology. A widely used environmental assessment and rating method for buildings.

CAD

Computer-aided design – software that allows 2D plans and 3D construction models to be created and designed on a computer.

Capital costs

The amount of money or goods a client has to spend at the outset of a project, as opposed to operational costs which are required to run and maintain a building project.

CDPs

Contractor's designed portions – commonly used in JCT contract agreements to allow a contractor to take responsibility for the design of pre-agreed parts of the project, allowing them to subcontract the design responsibility to specialist subcontractors.

CGI

Computer generated images are created by the application of computer graphics to create images/drawings within the computer media and design field.

Collaboration

Working with a group of people to discuss and exchange ideas to achieve a shared goal within a project.

Cost estimate

An approximate cost of a project, programme or operation within a business which is derived from a cost estimating process based on an appropriate level of available information.

Escher triangle

The Escher triangle is a representation of an impossible object – it has been referenced here because it symbolises the challenges faced in balancing three conflicting criteria – cost, quality and time. It is generally accepted that, in the design process, only two out of the three goals can be fully achieved.

Gantt chart

A horizontal chart, also known as a bar chart, that allows the project lead to schedule out a set of project activities in the correct sequence, applying logic links between dependencies. It is used to illustrate how much time will be required to complete a project.

Lead designer

On most building projects, the lead designer is usually the architect, unless the project is infrastructure or highly serviced. The lead designer's role predominantly involves defining the design process from inception to completion and, where there is no design manager, communicating and managing that process. As the name suggests, the lead designer is also the party responsible for developing and coordinating the inputs of all members of the design team and is the liaison with the client on issues relating to design.

Life cycle assessment

A technique that assesses the total life cycle costs and maintenance requirements of a project from inception to eventual demolition.

Lump sum

A projection of a total amount of money to be agreed in one single action instead of being divided and defined over a time period.

Milestones

A series of significant stages or events within a project's life cycle represented by key dates.

Operating and maintenance (O&M) manuals

This information (either hard copy or electronic) details the day-to-day procedures required for the safe and efficient operation and maintenance of the building's systems, as well as references to applicable codes and standards. The manuals are also useful for training and employee orientation.

Plan of work

A plan guiding a project and outlining how it is to be carried out; it details how the lead designer or design management team will outline the design activities within each stage of the project.

PPE

Personal protective equipment is equipment or clothing required to be worn under current health and safety legislation. This includes, among other things: Hi-Vis outer garments, steel toe-capped boots, protective glasses and gloves.

Procurement

Procurement is the process by which something is purchased and applies to the process in place to assemble both the design team and select the contractor.

Stakeholder

Stakeholders are third parties with either an interest in or an influence over the emerging design.

Tender

An offer made in response to a request for prices from a client. The tender documentation will contain detailed design information, terms and conditions and the specific requirements of a contract.

RIBA Plan of Work 2013 glossary

A number of new themes and subject matters have been included in the RIBA Plan of Work 2013. The following presents a glossary of all of the capitalised terms that are used throughout the RIBA Plan of Work 2013. Defining certain terms has been necessary to clarify the intent of a term, to provide additional insight into the purpose of certain terms and to ensure consistency in the interpretation of the RIBA Plan of Work 2013.

'As-constructed' Information

Information produced at the end of a project to represent what has been constructed. This will comprise a mixture of 'as-built' information from specialist subcontractors and the 'final construction issue' from design team members. Clients may also wish to undertake 'as-built' surveys using new surveying technologies to bring a further degree of accuracy to this information.

Building Contract

The contract between the client and the contractor for the construction of the project. In some instances, the **Building Contract** may contain design duties for specialist subcontractors and/or design team members. On some projects, more than one Building Contract may be required; for example, one for shell and core works and another for furniture, fitting and equipment aspects.

Building Information Modelling (BIM)

BIM is widely used as the acronym for 'Building Information Modelling', which is commonly defined (using the Construction Project Information Committee (CPIC) definition) as: 'digital representation of physical and functional characteristics of a facility creating a shared knowledge resource for information about it and forming a reliable basis for decisions during its life cycle, from earliest conception to demolition'.

Business Case

The **Business Case** for a project is the rationale behind the initiation of a new building project. It may consist solely of a reasoned argument. It may contain supporting information, financial appraisals or other background information. It should also highlight initial considerations for the **Project Outcomes**. In summary, it is a combination of objective and subjective considerations. The **Business Case** might be prepared in relation to, for example, appraising a number of sites or in relation to assessing a refurbishment against a new build option.

Change Control Procedures

Procedures for controlling changes to the design and construction following the sign-off of the Stage 2 Concept Design and the **Final Project Brief**.

Common Standards

Publicly available standards frequently used to define project and design management processes in relation to the briefing, designing, constructing, maintaining, operating and use of a building.

Communication Strategy

The strategy that sets out when the project team will meet, how they will communicate effectively and the protocols for issuing information between the various parties, both informally and at Information Exchanges.

Construction Programme

The period in the **Project Programme** and the **Building Contract** for the construction of the project, commencing on the site mobilisation date and ending at **Practical Completion**.

Construction Strategy

A strategy that considers specific aspects of the design that may affect the buildability or logistics of constructing a project, or may affect health and safety aspects. The **Construction Strategy** comprises items such as cranage, site access and accommodation locations, reviews of the supply chain and sources of materials, and specific buildability items, such as the choice of frame (steel or concrete) or the installation of larger items of plant. On a smaller project, the strategy may be restricted to the location of site cabins and storage, and the ability to transport materials up an existing staircase.

Contractor's Proposals

Proposals presented by a contractor to the client in response to a tender that includes the **Employer's Requirements**. The **Contractor's Proposals** may match the **Employer's Requirements**, although certain aspects may be varied based on value engineered solutions and additional information may be submitted to clarify what is included in the tender. The **Contractor's Proposals** form an integral component of the **Building Contract** documentation.

Contractual Tree

A diagram that clarifies the contractual relationship between the client and the parties undertaking the roles required on a project.

Cost Information

All of the project costs, including the cost estimate and life cycle costs where required.

Design Programme

A programme setting out the strategic dates in relation to the design process. It is aligned with the **Project Programme** but is strategic in its nature, due to the iterative nature of the design process, particularly in the early stages.

Design Queries

Queries relating to the design arising from the site, typically managed using a contractor's in-house request for information (RFI) or technical query (TQ) process.

Design Responsibility Matrix

A matrix that sets out who is responsible for designing each aspect of the project and when. This document sets out the extent of any performance specified design. The **Design Responsibility Matrix** is created at a strategic level at Stage 1 and fine tuned in response to the Concept Design at the end of Stage 2 in order to ensure that there are no design responsibility ambiguities at Stages 3, 4 and 5.

Employer's Requirements

Proposals prepared by design team members. The level of detail will depend on the stage at which the tender is issued to the contractor. The **Employer's Requirements** may comprise a mixture of prescriptive elements and descriptive elements to allow the contractor a degree of flexibility in determining the **Contractor's Proposals**.

Feasibility Studies

Studies undertaken on a given site to test the feasibility of the **Initial Project Brief** on a specific site or in a specific context and to consider how site-wide issues will be addressed.

Feedback

Feedback from the project team, including the end users, following completion of a building.

Final Project Brief

The **Initial Project Brief** amended so that it is aligned with the Concept Design and any briefing decisions made during Stage 2. (Both the Concept Design and **Initial Project Brief** are Information Exchanges at the end of Stage 2.)

Handover Strategy

The strategy for handing over a building, including the requirements for phased handovers, commissioning, training of staff or other factors crucial to the successful occupation of a building. On some projects, the Building Services Research and Information Association (BSRIA) Soft Landings process is used as the basis for formulating the strategy and undertaking a **Post-occupancy Evaluation** (www.bsria. co.uk/services/design/soft-landings/).

Health and Safety Strategy

The strategy covering all aspects of health and safety on the project, outlining legislative requirements as well as other project initiatives, including the **Maintenance and Operational Strategy**.

Information Exchange

The formal issue of information for review

and sign-off by the client at key stages of the project. The project team may also have additional formal **Information Exchanges** as well as the many informal exchanges that occur during the iterative design process.

Initial Project Brief

The brief prepared following discussions with the client to ascertain the **Project Objectives**, the client's **Business Case** and, in certain instances, in response to site **Feasibility Studies**.

Maintenance and Operational Strategy

The strategy for the maintenance and operation of a building, including details of any specific plant required to replace components.

Post-occupancy Evaluation

Evaluation undertaken post occupancy to determine whether the **Project Outcomes**, both subjective and objective, set out in the **Final Project Brief** have been achieved.

Practical Completion

Practical Completion is a contractual term used in the **Building Contract** to signify the date on which a project is handed over to the client. The date triggers a number of contractual mechanisms.

Project Budget

The client's budget for the project, which may include the construction cost as well as the cost of certain items required post completion and during the project's operational use.

Project Execution Plan

The **Project Execution Plan** is produced in collaboration between the project lead and lead designer, with contributions from other designers and members of the project team. The **Project Execution Plan** sets out the processes and protocols to be used to develop the design. It is sometimes referred to as a project quality plan.

Project Information

Information, including models, documents, specifications, schedules and spreadsheets, issued between parties during each stage and in formal Information Exchanges at the end of each stage.

Project Objectives

The client's key objectives as set out in the **Initial Project Brief**. The document includes, where appropriate, the employer's **Business Case**, **Sustainability Aspirations** or other aspects that may influence the preparation of the brief and, in turn, the Concept Design stage. For example, **Feasibility Studies** may be required in order to test the **Initial Project Brief** against a given site, allowing certain high-level briefing issues to be considered before design work commences in earnest.

Project Outcomes

The desired outcomes for the project (for example, in the case of a hospital this might be a reduction in recovery times). The outcomes may include operational aspects and a mixture of subjective and objective criteria.

Project Performance

The performance of the project, determined using **Feedback**, including about the performance of the project team and the performance of the building against the desired **Project Outcomes**.

Project Programme

The overall period for the briefing, design, construction and post-completion activities of a project.

Project Roles Table

A table that sets out the roles required on a project as well as defining the stages during which those roles are required and the parties responsible for carrying out the roles.

Project Strategies

The strategies developed in parallel with the Concept Design to support the design and, in certain instances, to respond to the **Final Project Brief** as it is concluded. These strategies typically include:

I   acoustic strategy
I   fire engineering strategy
I   **Maintenance and Operational Strategy**
I   **Sustainability Strategy**
I   building control strategy
I   **Technology Strategy.**

These strategies are usually prepared in outline at Stage 2 and in detail at Stage 3, with the recommendations absorbed into the Stage 4 outputs and Information Exchanges.

The strategies are not typically used for construction purposes because they may contain recommendations or information that contradict the drawn information. The intention is that they should be transferred into the various models or drawn information.

Quality Objectives

The objectives that set out the quality aspects of a project. The objectives may comprise both subjective and objective aspects, although subjective aspects may be subject to a design quality indicator (DQI) benchmark review during the **Feedback** period.

Research and Development

Project-specific research and development responding to the **Initial Project Brief** or in response to the Concept Design as it is developed.

Risk Assessment

The **Risk Assessment** considers the various design and other risks on a project and how each risk will be managed and the party responsible for managing each risk.

Schedule of Services

A list of specific services and tasks to be undertaken by a party involved in the project which is incorporated into their professional services contract.

Site Information

Specific **Project Information** in the form of specialist surveys or reports relating to the project- or site-specific context.

Strategic Brief

The brief prepared to enable the Strategic Definition of the project. Strategic considerations might include considering different sites, whether to extend, refurbish or build new and the key **Project Outcomes** as well as initial considerations for the **Project Programme** and assembling the project team.

Sustainability Aspirations

The client's aspirations for sustainability, which may include additional objectives, measures or specific levels of performance in relation to international standards, as well as details of specific demands in relation to operational or facilities management issues.

The **Sustainability Strategy** will be prepared in response to the **Sustainability Aspirations** and will include specific additional items, such as an energy plan and ecology plan and the design life of the building, as appropriate.

Sustainability Strategy

The strategy for delivering the **Sustainability Aspirations**.

Technology Strategy

The strategy established at the outset of a project that sets out technologies, including Building Information Modelling (BIM) and any supporting processes, and the specific software packages that each member of the project team will use. Any interoperability issues can then be addressed before the design phases commence.

This strategy also considers how information is to be communicated (by email, file transfer protocol (FTP) site or using a managed third party common data environment) as well as the file formats in which information will provided. The **Project Execution Plan** records agreements made.

Work in Progress

Work in Progress is ongoing design work that is issued between designers to facilitate the iterative coordination of each designer's output. Work issued as **Work in Progress** is signed off by the internal design processes of each designer and is checked and coordinated by the lead designer.

Index

Note: page numbers in italics refer to figures; page numbers in bold refer to tables.